SpringerBriefs in Service Science

T0406477

SpringerBriefs present concise summaries of cutting-edge research and practical applications across a wide spectrum of fields. Featuring compact volumes of 50 to 125 pages, the series covers a range of content from professional to academic.

Typical publications can be:

A timely report of state-of-the art methods

A bridge between new research results, as published in journal articles

A snapshot of a hot or emerging topic

An in-depth case study

A presentation of core concepts that students must understand in order to make independent contributions

SpringerBriefs are characterized by fast, global electronic dissemination, standard publishing contracts, standardized manuscript preparation and formatting guidelines, and expedited production schedules.

The rapidly growing fields of Big Data, AI and Machine Learning, together with emerging analytic theories and technologies, have allowed us to gain comprehensive insights into both social and transactional interactions in service value co-creation processes. The series SpringerBriefs in Service Science is devoted to publications that offer new perspectives on service research by showcasing service transformations across various sectors of the digital economy. The research findings presented will help service organizations address their service challenges in tomorrow's service-oriented economy.

Parminder Singh Kang • Xiaojia Wang
Joong Y. Son • Mohsin Jat

Service 4.0

Technology-Enabled Customer-Centric Supply Chains

 Springer

Parminder Singh Kang
MacEwan University
Edmonton, Canada

Joong Y. Son
MacEwan University
Edmonton, Canada

Xiaojia Wang
MacEwan University
Edmonton, Canada

Mohsin Jat
Thompson Rivers University
Kamloops, BC, Canada

ISSN 2731-3743   ISSN 2731-3751   (electronic)
SpringerBriefs in Service Science
ISBN 978-3-031-63874-9   ISBN 978-3-031-63875-6   (eBook)
https://doi.org/10.1007/978-3-031-63875-6

This Springer imprint is published by the registered company Springer Nature Switzerland AG
The registered company address is: Gewerbestrasse 11, 6330 Cham, Switzerland

If disposing of this product, please recycle the paper.

Preface

Welcome to a journey through the dynamic intersection of supply chain management, digitization, and the evolution of customer-centric services. In the wake of unprecedented disruptions like the global pandemic, organizations faced the imperative to transform supply chains. *The solution? Embrace the digital revolution.*

This book unveils a systematic framework for Service 4.0, a transformative concept at the core of the Supply Chain 4.0 revolution. Picture a landscape where cutting-edge technologies—like the Internet of Things (IoT), Big Data Analytics, Artificial Intelligence (AI), Machine Learning, and Blockchain Technologies—collide to reshape business operations and create resilient, customer-driven experiences.

We delve into real-world examples to illustrate the profound impact of digital adoption. The journey spans e-commerce giants such as Amazon, innovative food delivery platforms (Uber, SkipTheDishes), and the fast-food sector (McDonald's, Starbucks). Additionally, we examine a real dataset, showcasing how various data visualization and data mining methods unveil meaningful insights from historical data.

Join us as we explore the thrilling terrain of Service 4.0—a realm where the digital and physical seamlessly converge to redefine the future of supply chain management. This book is a valuable resource for scholars, practitioners, and students seeking to explore the evolving role of digital technologies in shaping customer-centric service-based supply chains.

As readers delve into the chapters ahead, envision a world where technology transcends being a mere tool and becomes the driving force behind innovative customer experiences and operational excellence. This book aims to stimulate the reader's curiosity, challenge perspectives, and inspire proactive engagement with the transformative potential of Service 4.0. Embark on this transformative journey with us and may "Service 4.0" be your guide in exploring the boundless possibilities at the intersection of technology and customer-centric supply chains.

Edmonton, AB, Canada — Parminder Singh Kang
Edmonton, AB, Canada — Xiaojia Wang
Edmonton, AB, Canada — Joong Y. Son
Kamloops, BC, Canada — Mohsin Jat

Contents

Abbreviations

AWS	Amazon Web Services
AI	Artificial Intelligence
AR	Augmented Reality
ARIMA	Auto-Regressive Integrated Moving Average
BD	Big Data
BDA	Big Data Analytics
BdaaS	Big Data-as-a-Service
BaaS	Blockchain-as-a-Service
BCT	Blockchain Technology
BOPIS	Buy Online, Pick Up In-Store
B2B	Business-to-business
B2C	Business-to-consumer
CAGR	Compound Annual Growth Rate
CAD	Computer Aided Design
CCSSC	Customer-Centric Service-Based Supply Chains
CCSC	Customer-Centric Supply Chains
CRM	Customer Relationship Management
CPS	Cyber-Physical Systems
DBMS	Database Management Systems
DDoS	Distributed Denial-of-Service
XR	Extended Reality
HDFS	Hadoop Distributed File System
HTML	Hypertext Markup Language
IoT	Internet of Things
JSON	JavaScript Object Notation
LLM	Large Language Model
LATR	Large-Scale Automated Test and Reorder
ML	Machine Learning
MINLP	Mixed Integer and Nonlinear Programming
MR	Mixed Reality
NLP	Natural Language Processing

ORION   On-Road Integrated Optimization and Navigation
PPT   People, Process, and Technology
POS   Point-of-Sale
RFID   Radio Frequency Identification
RM   Returns Management
SMEs   Small and Medium-sized Enterprises
SPSS   Smart Product Service Systems
SKU   Stock-keeping Unit
SC   Supply Chain
SCM   Supply Chain Management
SCRM   Supply Chain Risk Management
SRM   Supplier Relationship Management
VR   Virtual Reality
VOC   Voice of the Customer
WWF   World Wildlife Fund
XML   Extensible Markup Language
ZKP   Zero-Knowledge Proof

List of Figures

List of Tables

Chapter 1
Introduction to Service 4.0 and Customer-Centric Supply Chains

1.1 Service 4.0 and Customer-Centric Supply Chains of the Future: Evolution and Key Terms

The term "4.0" was first used in 2011 and is primarily linked to the fourth industrial revolution (Industry 4.0). The German government introduced Industry 4.0 as a strategic initiative to transform manufacturing through digitization. Industry 4.0 is primarily characterized by applying digital technologies to integrate the company's value chain to create fully integrated cyber-physical systems (CPS) [2, 3]. Industry 4.0 integrates advanced manufacturing techniques and innovative digital technologies to develop intelligent manufacturing systems that can communicate, analyze, predict, and use this real-time information to prescribe intelligent actions. From a systems perspective, modern SCs represent a complex web of customers and suppliers that relies on providing products and services to both upstream and downstream customers. With increased connectivity through digital technologies, the amount of data across SCs is growing exponentially. Organizations can leverage this data and information to develop innovative products, services, and business models to develop CCSCs of the future, with service as a critical component. Like Industry 4.0, CCSCs can package digital technologies and innovative service business models (Service 4.0) to provide tailored, agile, trustworthy, and innovative services:

- *Tailored*: Delivering customized products and services to meet each customer's specific needs.
- *Agile*: Possessing the ability to adjust and change to keep up with continually evolving customer demands.
- *Trustworthy*: Supporting transparency, traceability, and responsible behavior across the end-to-end value chain.
- *Innovative*: Continually attracting and delighting customers and bringing new and relevant products and services to the market.

P. S. Kang et al., *Service 4.0*, SpringerBriefs in Service Science, https://doi.org/10.1007/978-3-031-63875-6_1

1.2   Service 4.0: Design Principles

This section describes foundational concepts related to Service 4.0 design principles, primarily derived from Industry 4.0, to develop a better understanding of CPS interactions.

- *Decentralization*: Decentralization enables CPS to make decisions and trigger actions autonomously. Decentralization supports a faster decision-making process and improves the system's productivity, agility, and flexibility [3]. Modern organizations rely on the Internet of Things (IoT), sensors, and edge devices to collect data, share information, and control physical processes across the value chain. This also enables ubiquitous (anywhere, anytime) service delivery across the value chain [4]. The decentralization principle is crucial to Service 4.0 as it decomposes the classical centralized service-based models to promote autonomous decision-making with increased transparency. Some examples include Uber, Lyft, Etsy, Airbnb, and public/private blockchain networks.
- *Virtualization*: Cyber-physical interaction is an important aspect of the Service 4.0 process to monitor the physical process with its virtual copy [5]. For instance, logistics service providers, such as Uber, DoorDash, and SkipTheDishes, enable virtualization by providing real-time information from different sources such as service providers, service seekers, third-party service enablers (Google Maps), and regulatory bodies to enrich the experiences and decision-making capabilities of involved parties.
- *Interoperability*: Interoperability allows seamless communication between CPS entities. Applying new technologies, such as IoT devices, edge devices, sensors, and data fusion, helps achieve human–human, machine–human, and machine–machine interaction. Different components of a CPS play an important role in achieving the system's objective [2, 6]. For instance, for an Uber service, the request is generated from a person at a given location (physical entities), the request is processed to create a match with the available service provider, and payment is processed once the service is completed. In this high-level process, there is an interaction between humans, physical devices (mobile devices, GPS, etc.), and the technology infrastructure used to support the CPS interactions.
- *Modularity:* The concept of modularity has its roots in manufacturing, and its application evolved from products to services [7]. In the service domain, modularity refers to decomposing the total service offering into multiple, largely independent parts, so-called modules [8]. Businesses can better focus on their core value-creation modules by standardizing common sub-processes. Modularity is a foundation for achieving on-demand product differentiation, delivery flexibility, and personalized customer experience efficiently and effectively. For example, early application of modularity includes cruise service being modularized into various service segments such as cabin, food and beverage operations, swimming pools, entertainment, and engine room [9]. The current omnichannel trend also suggests that retailers with a brick-and-mortar store and an e-commerce website offer a buy online, pick up in-store (BOPIS) option. To efficiently

execute the BOPIS strategy, retailers divide their logistics services into modules to manage sub-processes directly affecting customer experiences, such as order receiving, order fulfillment, and inventory management.

- *Real-time capability:* Real-time capability refers to the ability of systems and devices to process and analyze data in real time, make decisions, and take actions in a timely manner. Integrating advanced technologies, such as the IoT, enables real-time data collection, processing, and analysis, allowing for real-time decision-making and action-taking.
- *Ubiquity:* Ubiquity refers to the ability of services to be available and accessible at any time and from anywhere through any device or platform. Technologies like cloud computing, edge devices, and IoT devices enable services to be delivered and accessed from anywhere, anytime, through any device or platform. Ubiquity allows for greater flexibility and convenience for customers and the ability for service providers to reach a wider audience. With cloud-based technologies, services can be delivered over the Internet in a user-friendly environment without the need for additional physical infrastructure. This allows customers to search for information or products, make selections, and complete purchases through mobile devices. Businesses can also leverage data generated from product searches, locations, purchases, etc., to understand customer behavior, needs, and preferences.
- *Superior expertise and delivery*: Superior expertise and delivery are key design principles for Service 4.0 that can enhance customer satisfaction and loyalty. Service 4.0 requires companies to leverage advanced technologies such as AI, big data analytics (BDA), and IoT devices to improve service offerings by providing personalized services that meet customers' needs and preferences [10, 11]. Several aspects of "superior expertise and delivery" make it a critical part of Service 4.0, such as enhancing customer satisfaction by delivering accurate and timely service delivery on a consistent basis, building customer loyalty by analyzing the digital trail and spending patterns, and increasing operational efficiency by using predictive analytics to anticipate customer needs. This can promote greater customization of service offerings through web-based interfaces, edge devices, data analytics, and other tools. Companies are already leveraging this design principle; for example, Sephora is a beauty retailer that uses Service 4.0 to enhance its customer experience. Sephora has developed a mobile app that uses augmented reality to help customers try on makeup virtually. Customers can scan their faces with the app and then apply virtual makeup to see how it would look. This provides customers with a personalized experience that enhances their satisfaction with the brand [12]. Other examples include Nike's mobile app that uses AI to analyze customers' fitness data and provide product recommendations based on their needs. This helps customers find products tailored to their specific needs and preferences, enhancing their satisfaction with the brand [13].
- *Computational intelligence:* Computational intelligence refers to the use of AI and machine learning (ML) techniques to enhance service delivery; as a crucial component of digital transformation, computational intelligence can help

businesses effectively utilize large volumes of structured and unstructured data generated through internal (internal processes, devices, databases, etc.) and external (social media, tracking devices, reviews, recommendations, etc.) sources. This can help organizations better understand customer preferences and the need to provide personalized service experiences. Also, organizations can leverage computational intelligence to automate and optimize service processes to reduce costs and improve operational efficiency.

1.3 Service 4.0 Enablers

This section explains nine Service 4.0 enabling technologies to improve service efficiency, effectiveness, transparency, and offerings [14].

- *Big data and analytics:* The Service 4.0 enabler "big data (BD) and analytics" refers to using large volumes of data and advanced analytics techniques to gain insights into customer behavior, preferences, and needs. This enabler facilitates businesses to develop more personalized and targeted service offerings tailored to individual customers. Businesses can identify patterns, trends, and opportunities to improve service delivery and customer satisfaction by collecting and analyzing data from various sources [14, 15]. Examples in the service sector include Uber, which collects massive amounts of data from its riders and drivers, including their locations, trip durations, ratings, and more. Analysis of this data leads to gaining insights into customer behavior and preferences, such as preferred pickup locations and ride routes. Delivery companies like Uber can optimize service delivery by reducing wait times, improving route efficiency, and offering targeted promotions and incentives to customers. Similarly, by analyzing customer purchase history, search queries, and browsing behavior, Amazon can recommend products and services tailored to each customer's needs and preferences. This increases customer satisfaction and loyalty, as customers feel that Amazon understands their needs and offers relevant products and services.
- *Cloud computing:* The Service 4.0 enabler "cloud computing" refers to using remote servers hosted on the Internet to store, manage, and process data. This enabler allows businesses to access computing resources on demand without significant investments in physical infrastructure. With cloud computing, businesses can easily scale their service offerings, improve operational efficiency, and reduce costs [16, 17]. Companies like Uber use cloud computing to manage their vast network of drivers and riders and support their apps and websites. By leveraging cloud computing, Uber can easily scale its operations to meet the demands of its customers without the need to invest in physical infrastructure. Similarly, companies like Amazon also heavily rely on cloud computing to support their e-commerce platform. Amazon's cloud computing service, Amazon Web Services (AWS), provides the company with scalable and flexible computing

resources that can be used to support a wide range of services, including its online marketplace and Prime Video streaming service.

- *Robotics and process automation:* The Service 4.0 enabler "robotics and process automation" refers to using robots and automated processes to perform tasks traditionally done by humans [14, 18]. This enabler allows businesses to improve efficiency, reduce costs, and enhance the quality of service. By automating routine tasks, businesses can free up their employees to focus on higher-value tasks, such as customer service and problem-solving. Companies like Amazon are already leveraging these automation capabilities by using robots in their warehouses to handle tasks such as picking, packing, and shipping orders. The robots work alongside human workers to increase efficiency and speed up the fulfillment process [19]. Amazon also developed a fleet of delivery drones to deliver packages directly to customers' homes. This delivery process automation can reduce delivery times and costs and improve overall customer satisfaction. Similarly, Uber's use of self-driving cars is an example of using robotics and automation to transport passengers without needing a human driver. Although still in development, the use of self-driving cars has the potential to reduce the cost of transportation and improve safety significantly.
- *Cognitive computing:* Cognitive computing is another enabler of Service 4.0, which involves using advanced technologies such as AI, ML, and natural language processing (NLP) to simulate human thought processes. This allows businesses to gain insights into customer needs and preferences, automate routine tasks, and improve customer experience [20]. Overall, cognitive computing is an essential enabler of Service 4.0 because it allows businesses to leverage the power of advanced technologies to improve the quality and efficiency of service delivery and enhance the overall customer experience. Amazon's Alexa virtual assistant is an example of how cognitive computing can be used to improve customer experience. Alexa uses NLP and ML to understand and respond to customer queries and commands, making it easier for customers to find and order products. Similarly, Uber uses ML algorithms to predict rider demand and driver availability in different locations, allowing it to dispatch drivers more efficiently and reduce customer wait times [21]. Uber also uses NLP to enable customers to hail rides using voice commands through its mobile app.
- *Extended reality:* Extended reality (XR) refers to a fusion of technologies that enable virtual environments or experiences by real-world scenarios. It is an umbrella term encompassing augmented reality (AR), virtual reality (VR), and mixed reality (MR) to create immersive experiences for customers. XR utilizes technologies such as sensors, cameras, head-mounted displays (such as Microsoft HoloLens), AI, and cloud computing to create digital immersive experiences. XR is closely linked to other enablers of Service 4.0, such as cloud computing, big data and analytics, and cognitive computing, as it relies on creating virtual environments to deliver services and analyze data. Through XR, customers can interact with products or services in a simulated environment without needing physical presence or interaction with real-world objects [22]. This can enhance the customer experience by providing a more engaging, personalized, and conve-

nient way of accessing products and services. During COVID-19, many retailers have adopted virtual shopping experiences, allowing customers to browse and purchase products online through virtual showrooms, AR apps, and VR experiences. This has enabled retailers to continue engaging with customers and providing personalized experiences, even when physical stores were closed. One notable example of AR is IKEA's AR app, which revolutionizes furniture shopping. With this app, users can virtually place furniture pieces from IKEA's catalog into their living spaces using smartphones or tablets. The latest app version, called IKEA Kreativ, allows users to add furniture and see how it would look and fit in homes and lets users virtually remove existing furniture to start with an empty room [25]. Other examples include Sephora's virtual artist,[1] Zyler Try On Outfits,[2] McDonald's McMission,[3] etc.

- *Ubiquitous connectivity and IoT:* Ubiquitous connectivity refers to the state where devices and systems can connect and communicate with each other seamlessly, anytime and anywhere, with minimum human intervention. This is enabled by the widespread availability of the Internet and other communication networks and the proliferation of IoT devices [23, 24]. In the context of Service 4.0, ubiquitous connectivity and IoT devices can enable the collection of real-time data from various sources, such as customer behaviors and preferences, product usage patterns, and SC performance. This data can then be analyzed and used to improve and personalize the customer experience, optimize operational efficiency, and drive innovation in service delivery. For example, Uber utilizes IoT technology, particularly in their ride-hailing platform. The Uber app uses GPS and location-based services to connect riders with nearby drivers and provide real-time information on the estimated time of arrival and fare estimates.

- *Smart edge devices:* Smart edge devices refer to the hardware and software technologies that enable the collection, processing, and analysis of data at the edge of a network or device. These devices have sensors, processors, and communication capabilities, allowing them to perform tasks autonomously and communicate with other devices and networks in real time [23]. Devices such as smart thermostats, smart security cameras, wearable devices, smart appliances, and industrial sensors can capture and transmit data on temperature, humidity, motion, location, and other environmental factors. For instance, Uber uses GPS and sensors to track locations and monitor driving behaviors. This data is then used to optimize routes, provide real-time traffic updates, and enhance overall safety and efficiency for both drivers and riders [21].

---

[1] https://www.sephora.sg/pages/virtual-artist.

[2] https://www.zyler.com/shoppers/lookbooks/clubl.

[3] https://www.packworld.com/home/news/13363086/mcmission-ar-app-promotes-mcdonalds-sustainability-efforts.

1.4 Service 4.0 as a Key Facilitator to Customer-Centric Supply Chains of the Future

The past few decades have seen a significant shift and expansion of manufacturers into the service domain by providing product-linked services. A manufacturer's venture into the service domain, widely termed as servitization, offers several benefits. Product-linked services allow manufacturers to earn revenue after sales while providing assurance and convenience to customers during the product life. Due to continued interaction with customers and an element of value co-creation with customers, servitized manufacturers can provide better responses to customer requirements, perform customer-centric innovations, and attain greater customer loyalty. Besides these more direct benefits, service provision can improve supply chain risk management (SCRM) due to greater information-sharing elements in delivering services compared with the production of goods. Manufacturers must also realize that rather than a choice to attain financial and other performance-related benefits, offering product-linked services is likely to become a compulsion in contemporary SCs. The market dynamism characterized by rapid changes and higher technical complexities in products and processes can necessitate service provision for success in the market. Industry reports have suggested a nexus between digitization and servitization [26].

Service activities of a manufacturer not only increase the need for cooperation and knowledge sharing with customers but also create external dependencies that require alliances and collaborations with suppliers. Service 4.0, being underpinned by digitization, adoption of AI/ML/BDA, and the concept of "everything as a service," can play a crucial role in facilitating the customer-centricity aspirations of future SCs. Digitization and AI can allow rapid information gathering and sense-making of data and information captured downstream. The treatment of capabilities, products, and processes as a horizontal palette of services available across organizational boundaries in a SC can provide a seamless mechanism for acting on customer requirements in a timely and efficient manner. Figure 1.1 presents a stylized SC setup oriented toward serving customers based on the aforementioned principles. Real-time sense-making and a frictionless response to customer needs can mitigate the many disruptions posed by the complex and dynamic environment in which SCs operate. Timely data gathering, analysis, and information sharing with partners can also allow responsiveness in capturing and acting on customers' evolving preferences, including the ones related to product delivery, to serve the customers better. From this perspective, distribution logistics can also be considered as constituents of service infrastructure.

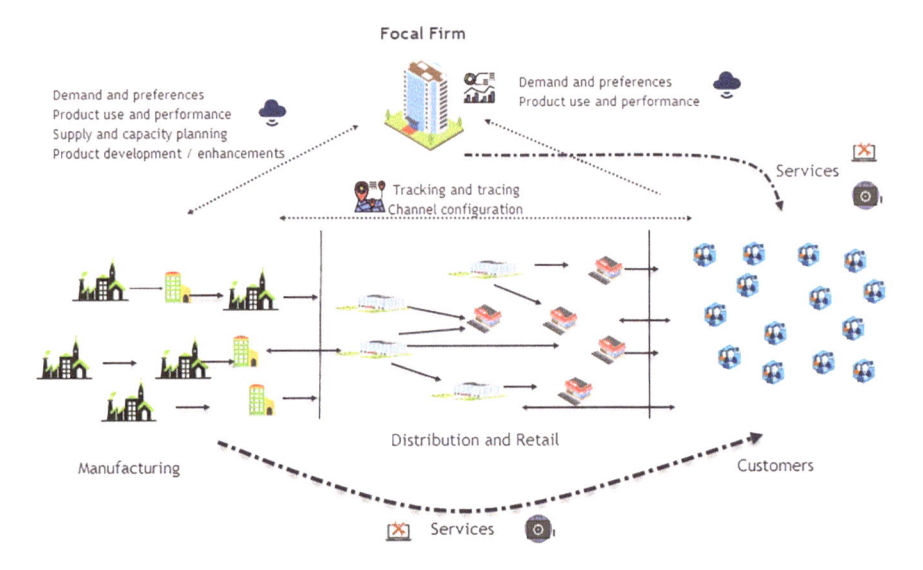

Fig. 1.1 Customer-centric supply chain driven by customer data

1.5   Pitfalls and Risks of Service 4.0

While manufacturers' venture into services has significant potential on various performance metrics, the service domain exposes manufacturers to several challenges. The term "servitization paradox" has been used to suggest that while value-creation opportunities from service provisions seem straightforward, the actual returns are not. Several studies have highlighted that servitization increases manufacturers' risk due to factors like the loss of strategic focus, the assumption of greater responsibility, and the required structural changes [26]. Designing and delivering services is complex, requiring alliances and collaboration with SC partners. Service 4.0 requires highly advanced capabilities, making alliances, collaborations, and SC cohesion even more critical. Although cooperation and integration are considered fundamental in supply chain management (SCM), achieving these is problematic as SC partners are independent entities with diverse internal and external contexts and technical capabilities. The majority of manufacturers are still not technically advanced. Specifically, the lack of standardization, where SC partners have very different levels of capabilities, can be a significant barrier to adopting Service 4.0. Another challenge in implementing Service 4.0 can be the customer's perception of automated and AI-based services. Studies have found that automated or technology-based service setups are perceived to be significantly lower in richness and not relationship-oriented [27]. While AI-powered automated services can provide convenience, services by personnel, which include the empathy factor and the capability to pay individualized attention to customers, are critical for customer satisfaction [28, 29]. Finally, the digitization and data sharing requirements of Service 4.0 can raise data security and privacy concerns for customers as well as the SC partners.

The movement of material and provision of services, even in traditional SCs, is managed through the flow of associated information. For example, commercial information is shared with advisors and consultants, and personally identifiable information about customers and intellectual property is shared with suppliers. A compromised transmission and use of this information can have significant implications [30]. By its very nature, the Service 4.0 framework amplifies information requirements and flow, increasing the potential for unauthorized information disclosure and data leakage.

References

1. Amankwah-Amoah, J., Khan, Z., & Wood, G. (2020). COVID-19 and business failures: The paradoxes of experience, scale and scope for theory and practice. *European Management Journal, 39*(2), 179–184. https://doi.org/10.1016/j.emj.2020.09.002
2. Rojko, A. (2017). Industry 4.0 concept: Background and overview. *International Journal of Interactive Mobile Technologies, 11*(5), 77–90. https://doi.org/10.3991/ijim.v11i5.7072
3. Roblek, V., Meško, M., & Krapež, A. (2016). A complex view of industry 4.0. *SAGE Journals, 6*(2), 1–11. https://doi.org/10.1177/2158244016653987
4. Deloitte, A. G. (2015). Industry 4.0: Challenges and solutions for the digital transformation and use of exponential technologies. Available online: https://www2.deloitte.com/content/dam/Deloitte/ch/Documents/manufacturing/ch-en-manufacturing-industry-4-0-241-02014.pdf
5. Hermann, M., Pentek, T., & Otto, B. (2016). Design principles for industry 4.0 scenarios. In *2016 49th Hawaii international conference on system sciences (HICSS), Koloa, HI, USA* (pp. 3928–3937). https://doi.org/10.1109/HICSS.2016.488
6. Dikhanabayeva, D., Shaikholla, S., Suleiman, Z., & Turkyilmaz, A. (2020). Assessment of industry 4.0 maturity models by design principles. *Sustainability, 12*(23), 1–22. https://doi.org/10.3390/su12239927
7. Brax, S. A., Bask, A., Hsuan, J., & Voss, C. (2017). Service modularity and architecture—An overview and research agenda. *International Journal of Operations & Production Management., 37*(6), 686–702. https://doi.org/10.1108/IJOPM-03-2017-0191
8. Bartels, E. A., Meijboom, B. R., Nahar-van Venrooij, L. M. W., & de Vries, E. (2021). How service modularity can provide the flexibility to support person-centred care and shared decision-making. *BMC Health Services Research, 21*, 1245.
9. Voss, C. A., & Hsuan, J. (2009). Service architecture and modularity. *Decision Sciences, 40*(3), 541–569. https://doi.org/10.1111/j.1540-5915.2009.00241.x
10. IBM Services. (2018, October 2). Service 4.0 Paves the way for technology support transformation [Blog post]. Retrieved June 29, 2023, from https://www.ibm.com/blogs/services/2018/10/02/service-4-0-paves-the-way-for-technology-ssupport-transformation/
11. Lemon, K. N., & Verhoef, P. C. (2016). Understanding customer experience throughout the customer journey. *Journal of Marketing, 80*(6), 69–96. https://doi.org/10.1509/jm.15.0420
12. Sephora. (n.d.). Sephora virtual artist. Retrieved July 20, 2023, from https://www.sephora.sg/pages/virtual-artist
13. Schipani, C. (2019, October 7). How Nike is using analytics to personalize their customer experience. Forbes. Retrieved August 07, 2023, from https://www.forbes.com/sites/forbestechcouncil/2019/10/07/how-nike-is-using-analytics-to-personalize-their-customer-experience/?sh=7c5c493d1611
14. Rehse, O., Hoffmann, S., & Kosanke, C. (2016). Tapping into the transformative power of service 4.0. Retrieved May 20, 2023, from https://www.bcg.com/publications/2016/tapping-into-the-transformative-power-of-service-4

15. Amart-Lefort, N., Barravecchia, F., & Mastrogiacomo, L. (2022). Quality 4.0: Big data analytics to explore service quality attributes and their relation to user sentiment in Airbnb reviews. *International Journal of Quality & Reliability Management, 40*(4), 990–1008. https://doi.org/10.1108/ijqrm-01-2022-0024

16. Attaran, M., & Woods, J. (2019). Cloud computing technology: Improving small business performance using the internet. *Journal of Small Business & Entrepreneurship, 31*(6), 495–519. https://doi.org/10.1080/08276331.2018.1466850

17. Hashem, I. A. T., Yaqoob, I., Anuar, N. B., Mokhtar, S., Gani, A., & Khan, S. U. (2015). The rise of "big data" on cloud computing: Review and open research issues. *Information Systems, 47*(1), 98–115. https://doi.org/10.1016/j.is.2014.07.006

18. Afriliana, N., & Ramadhan, A. (2022). The trends and roles of robotic process automation technology in digital transformation: A literature review. *Journal of System and Management Sciences, 12*(3), 51–73. https://doi.org/10.1108/BPMJ-08-2022-0409

19. Knight, W. (2023). Amazon's new robots are rolling out an automation revolution. WIRED. Retrieved June 29, 2023, sfrom https://www.wired.com/story/amazons-new-robots-automation-revolution/

20. Google Cloud Topics. (n.d.). What is cognitive computing? Retrieved June 29, 2023, from https://cloud.google.com/discover/what-is-cognitive-computing

21. Uber Blog. (2019). Uber AI in 2019: Advancing mobility with artificial intelligence. Retrieved June 29, 2023, from https://www.uber.com/en-CA/blog/uber-ai-blog-2019/

22. Brettel, M., Friederichsen, N., Keller, M., & Rosenberg, M. (2014). How virtualization, decentralization and network building change the manufacturing landscape: An industry 4.0 perspective. *World Academy of Science, Engineering and Technology International Journal of Mechanical, Aerospace, Industrial, Mechatronic and Manufacturing Engineering., 8*(1), 37–44.

23. Nayyar, A., & Kumar, A. (eds.). (2020). Ubiquitous manufacturing in the age of industry 4.0: A state-of-the-art primer. *A roadmap to industry 4.0: Smart production, sharp business and sustainable development, advances in science, technology & innovation.* https://doi.org/10.1007/978-3-030-14544-6_5.

24. Shubhangini, R., & Surya, P. S. (2018). Identifying industry 4.0 IoT enablers by integrated PCA-ISM-DEMATEL approach. *Management Decision, 57*(8), 1784–1817. https://doi.org/10.1108/MD-04-2018-0378

25. Dent, S. (2022, June 22). IKEA's latest AR app can erase your furniture to showcase its own. [Blog post]. Retrieved September 20, 2023, from https://www.engadget.com/ikea-ar-app-lets-you-preview-its-furniture-in-your-own-house-130004284.html

26. Jat, M. N., Jajja, M. S. S., Shah, S. A. A., & Farooq, S. (2023). Manufacturer's servitization level and financial performance: The role of risk management. *Journal of Manufacturing Technology Management, 34*(1), 122–146. https://doi.org/10.1108/JMTM-12-2021-0503

27. Froehle, C. M. (2006). Service personnel, technology, and their interaction in influencing customer satisfaction. *Decision Sciences, 37*(1), 5–38. https://doi.org/10.1111/j.1540-5414.2006.00108.x

28. Prentice, C., Dominique Lopes, S., & Wang, X. (2020). The impact of artificial intelligence and employee service quality on customer satisfaction and loyalty. *Journal of Hospitality Marketing & Management, 29*(7), 739–756. https://doi.org/10.1080/19368623.2020.1722304

29. Wirtz, J., Patterson, P. G., Kunz, W. H., Gruber, T., Lu, V. N., Paluch, S., & Martins, A. (2018). Brave new world: Service robots in the frontline. *Journal of Service Management, 29*(5), 907–931. https://doi.org/10.1108/JOSM-04-2018-0119

30. Bhargava, B., Ranchal, R., & Othmane, L. B. (2013). Secure information sharing in digital supply shains. In *2013 3rd IEEE international advance computing conference (IACC), Ghaziabad, India* (pp. 1636–1640). https://doi.org/10.1109/IAdCC.2013.6514473

Chapter 2
Role of Big Data in Customer-Centric Service-Based Supply Chains

2.1 The Role of Service 4.0 Enablers in Customer-Centric Supply Chains

Global supply chains (SC) are complex and dynamic systems that involve coordinating many stakeholders, including suppliers, manufacturers, logistics providers, and retailers. These SCs span multiple countries and involve numerous regulatory and cultural challenges. To represent this complex, dynamic, and interconnected global SCs, the term "supply chain web" is used, encapsulating an extended and interconnected network of suppliers, manufacturers, distributors, retailers, and other entities involved in the SC process. In a SC web, multiple suppliers, manufacturers, and distributors may be interconnected, forming a web-like network of relationships and interactions. The SC web enables organizations to have multiple sourcing options, diverse manufacturing capabilities, and flexible distribution channels. It represents a more complex and interdependent structure than a traditional linear SC. For example, Amazon's SC involves a complex web of suppliers, manufacturers, and logistics providers worldwide. Amazon sources products from suppliers in countries like China, India, and the USA and works with logistics providers like UPS and FedEx to transport those products to warehouses and fulfillment centers worldwide. Amazon leverages big data analytics (BDA) extensively throughout its SC operations to enhance its customer-centric approach, focusing on advanced demand forecasting, personalized recommendations, SC and logistics optimization, customer feedback and social media analytics, returns management, etc. [1]. The real-time and dynamic information exchange among the SC through integrated cyber-physical systems (CPS) can lead to vertical and horizontal communication for an accurate business decision, multiparty collaboration, efficient and effective system improvements, and optimization. Several digital technologies introduced in Chap. 1 enable this interaction between CPS to generate, collect, and store large quantities of data of different formats in real time. By embracing Service 4.0,

P. S. Kang et al., *Service 4.0*, SpringerBriefs in Service Science, https://doi.org/10.1007/978-3-031-63875-6_2

organizations can transform their SCs into customer-centric ecosystems where personalized services, real-time responsiveness, and seamless experiences are at the forefront. It can help organizations understand and meet customer needs effectively, build long-term customer relationships, and differentiate themselves in the market by delivering superior service experiences. This chapter will explore CCSSC of the future concepts from the Service 4.0 lens, specifically focusing on BDA concepts and associated terminology.

2.2 Overview of Big Data and Data Analytics

The accelerated digitization across SCs has enabled different intra- and inter-organizational processes and subprocesses to be part of the global CPS. The interactions among these CPS entities generate massive amounts of structured, semi-structured, and unstructured datasets. The data collected from traditional (transaction data, customer data, sensor data, log files, machine-generated data, etc.) and nontraditional sources (social media, web, textual, multimedia, geospatial, etc.) in various formats can constitute BD. There are several definitions of BD; however, two definitions are provided to give a bigger picture to readers:

- Big data is high-volume, high-velocity, and/or high-variety information assets that demand cost-effective, innovative forms of information processing that enable enhanced insight, decision-making, and process automation [2].
- Big data combines Volume, Variety, Velocity, Veracity, and Value (5Vs—Table 2.1), creating an opportunity for organizations to gain a competitive advantage in today's digitized marketplace [3].

Larger organizations, like Walmart, already leverage BD and analytics to increase sales, profitability, and operational efficiency. For example, Walmart collects over 2.5 petabytes of unstructured data globally from its customers every hour from social media and website feeds to understand customer behavior, buying patterns, and trends. Additionally, the analysis is combined with the internal datasets from point-of-sales systems, inventory data, weather, supplier and store maps, etc., to optimize the product offerings, SC operations, and cost reduction through better predictive models [7].

Based on the BD definitions and characteristics, the BD concept can be summarized based on four key characteristics:

- *Information and knowledge generation*: Raw data is like crude oil; it needs to be processed and refined before being used as fuel through analytical engines to power data-driven business decisions in the form of information and knowledge. According to Statista [8, 9], the total data created, captured, and consumed globally is projected to grow to over 180 zettabytes, and there will be more than 29 billion IoT devices by 2030. The increasing availability of data from internal and

Table 2.1 5Vs of big data

Dimension	Description
Volume	Volume refers to the data size and scale, a relative concept that varies with the data type, data compression technology, data management, and storage capacities. BD is usually in the range of multiple terabytes and petabytes [4–6]. With increased IT capabilities and advanced digital technologies, more data can be stored by compressing different data types (text, video, audio, etc.) without losing the information
Variety	Modern organizations collect large volumes of multidimensional data from internal and external sources in structured, semi-structured, and unstructured formats—this refers to the BD dimension variety [4–6]. *Structured* data represents data stored in relational databases and spreadsheets in a tabular format with fixed fields—such as point-of-sales, inventory, demand data, etc. *Unstructured* data does not follow any predefined data format. It can take various forms, including text documents, emails, social media posts, images, videos, audio files, sensor data, etc. It is typically generated by humans or machines and does not conform to a rigid data structure. *Semi-structured* data falls between structured and unstructured data. It possesses structured and unstructured data elements, exhibiting some form of organization but not adhering to a rigid schema or predefined data model. Examples of semi-structured data include XML (extensible markup language), JSON (JavaScript object notation), and HTML (hypertext markup language)
Velocity	BD is generated at high speed and in real time or near real time. The data streams rapidly from various sources, such as social media feeds, IoT (Internet of Things) devices, sensors, and online transactions. Processing and analyzing data quickly are essential to derive valuable insights and make timely decisions [4–6]
Veracity	Veracity focuses on the quality and reliability of data. BD often includes data from multiple sources with varying degrees of accuracy and consistency—this makes BD ambiguous and dirty (unverified) data that needs to be cleaned and organized. Veracity encompasses data quality issues such as incompleteness, inconsistency, errors, and biases [4–6]. For instance, sentiment analysis of social media data requires dealing with the challenge of interpreting ambiguous or sarcastic posts. Analysis of such data may lead to misleading and false conclusions
Value	Value represents the ultimate goal of BD, which is to extract meaningful insights and derive value from the data. The value of BD lies in its ability to uncover patterns, trends, correlations, and actionable insights that can drive business decisions and innovation [4–6]. For example, analyzing customer data can reveal purchasing patterns, preferences, and trends, enabling businesses to personalize their marketing strategies and improve customer satisfaction

external sources can help organizations use advanced data-driven analytics approaches (Chap. 3) to create new products, services, and business models, optimize business processes, reduce cost and risk, and increase profits.

- *Technological innovation*: CCSSC enablers (Chap. 1), such as IoT devices, cloud computing, automation, and smart edge devices, allow real-time data capturing and processing. Distributed information capturing and analytics capabilities are key to seamless inter- and intra-process integration across CCSSC; for example, companies like Amazon, Starbucks, and Sheep Inc. leverage these capabilities to improve SC transparency and resilience.

- *Advanced data analytics approaches*: Advanced data analytics encompasses a range of sophisticated approaches designed to extract valuable insights from complex datasets. Machine learning (ML) is a key component involving algorithms that enable computers to learn patterns and make predictions autonomously. ML algorithms can also be used to process data types like images and text. Predictive analytics utilizes statistical algorithms and ML techniques to forecast future events, while prescriptive analytics suggests optimal actions to achieve desired outcomes. Natural Language Processing (NLP) facilitates interactions between computers and human language, applied in chatbots, sentiment analysis, and language translation. Time series analysis focuses on identifying patterns and trends in data collected over time, and association rule mining reveals relationships between variables. Cluster analysis groups similar data points, useful for customer segmentation and anomaly detection. Simulation and optimization create models to imitate real-world systems and find optimal logistics and resource allocation solutions [10].
- *Value and impact*: BD is useless unless utilized to empower individuals, businesses, and society through data-driven decisions. Examples of effective data-driven decision-making include SC optimization and personalized recommendations from Amazon. Better predictive and prescriptive models can be developed to align demand and supply by analyzing large volumes of SC data related to customer orders, inventory levels, transportation networks, and demand patterns. In Amazon's example, analysis of customers' browsing history, purchase behavior, and product preferences not only helps Amazon offer tailored product recommendations to individual customers but also enables them to position inventory in warehouses closer to customer locations strategically. Similarly, companies like Uber can adjust prices dynamically to match supply and demand by analyzing data on real-time demand, traffic conditions, driver availability, and other relevant factors. Using data from multiple sources, companies can create digital twins to understand the impact of assets on customers, business performance, and the environment. For instance, transportation companies can use data from various sensors installed in the vehicles, such as engine performance, tire pressure, oil quality, emissions, speed, and load, to develop proactive approaches to minimize vehicle breakdowns, improve safety, reduce emissions, and improve overall customer and service provider experience by minimizing service disruptions. Beyond individuals and businesses, BD can be utilized for crime prevention, emergency response optimization, and enhancing overall public safety measures. For example, technologies like ShotSpotter use a network of sensors and BDA to detect and locate gunshots in real time. The system analyzes audio signatures, time delays, and other factors to pinpoint the location of gunshots accurately.

2.3 Supply Chain Big Data Life Cycle and Ecosystem

BD is a critical part of the CCSSC, empowering organizations to understand their customers better, personalize services, make real-time decisions, optimize operations, and effectively manage inventory. By leveraging the power of data analytics, organizations can create CCSSCs that deliver superior experiences, drive customer loyalty, and gain a competitive edge in the marketplace. It also makes it a complex and challenging topic to understand the context of highly interconnected and interdependent global SCs. This section will focus on understanding the SC ecosystem under CPS dependencies and Service 4.0 principles based on the four interrelated aspects of SC web—SC structure and interactions, processes, flows, and digitization.

2.3.1 Digital Supply Chain Web

SC web allows organizations to leverage multiple partners, collaborate effectively, and adapt to dynamic market conditions, improving SC performance and customer satisfaction. The SC web for any organization relies on the CPS interactions through various cyber-physical processes to promote seamless integration and coordination of various physical and virtual flows. This involves seamless interactions among tier 1, 2, and 3 suppliers, manufacturing firms, logistics service providers, wholesalers, retailers, and end customers. One example of such complex interactions would be the integration of an e-commerce platform from an online retailer (such as Amazon) with its logistics network and suppliers enabled through cyber-physical processes and flows (the next two components of the SC web). To achieve a seamless customer experience with efficient order processing, reliable shipping, and responsive support, the CCSSC of the future requires coordination between various components, including demand management, sourcing, inventory management, fulfillment centers, logistics operations, and customer service. This coordination requires different supply chain management (SCM) processes such as customer relationship management (CRM), supplier relationship management (SRM), returns management (RM), customer service management, demand and inventory management, order fulfillment, production and operations, product development and research, and quality management and process improvement. All these processes contribute to the efficient flow of material, finished products, services, information, knowledge, financial flow, and returns through CPS interactions. This is where SC digitization and BDA come into play to promote data-driven decisions based on the information and knowledge generated by analyzing various SCM processes. Digitization has become more critical for the CCSSC of the future because of COVID-19. Digital adoption across SCs and most industries has shown exponential growth, accelerated the digitization of products and services, and contributed toward the exponential growth of data across SCs.

Digital SCs can be defined as intelligent best-fit technological CPS based on the capability of BDA and advanced digital technologies to support and synchronize interaction between SC web entities by making services more valuable, accessible, and affordable with consistent, agile, and effective outcomes [11].

The CPS interactions contributing toward data, information, and knowledge can be further explained based on the process of a customer placing an order for a hypothetical online retailer (e.g., RetailerX in Fig. 2.1):

- *Customer order*: A customer visits the RetailerX website or mobile app and places an order for a product. At this stage, semi-structured data about the customer's order is generated, including the product details, quantity, price, and any additional specifications or preferences provided by the customer. BDA can be utilized to analyze this data to understand customer preferences, identify popular products, and make personalized recommendations.
- *Inventory management*: Once the order is received, RetailerX's digital system checks the product's availability in its inventory across various distribution centers or fulfillment centers. This involves real-time inventory tracking and allocation. At this stage, structured data regarding the product's availability is produced from different distribution centers. This includes information about the quantity of the product in stock, its location in various distribution centers, and any variations in availability over time. BDA can analyze this data to optimize inventory levels, identify demand patterns, and ensure timely restocking to meet future customer demands.

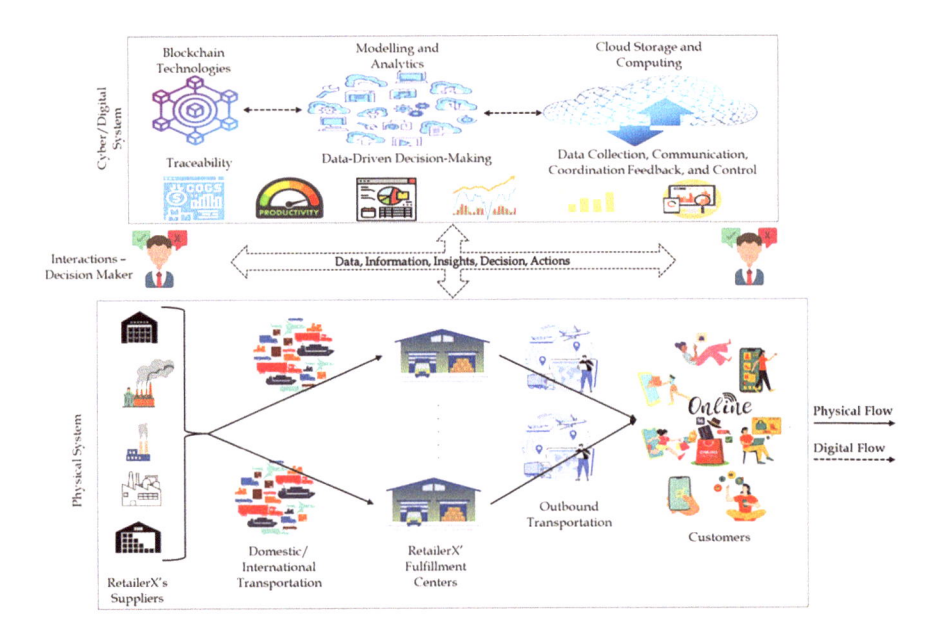

Fig. 2.1 CPS Interactions—RetailerX

- *Fulfillment*: If the product is available in a nearby fulfillment center, the order is routed to that center for packing and shipping. However, if the product is unavailable, RetailerX's system identifies the nearest location where the product is in stock. Data is generated during the fulfillment process, including routing the order to the appropriate fulfillment center, packing details, and inventory allocation for the specific order. BDA can optimize the allocation of orders to fulfillment centers, track packing efficiency, and identify bottlenecks in the fulfillment process.
- *Shipping and logistics*: RetailerX's logistics network comes into play to ensure efficient and timely delivery. The system determines the best shipping method based on customer location, delivery speed, and cost optimization. It may involve RetailerX's own delivery fleet, third-party logistics partners, or a combination of both. Data, such as the chosen shipping method, transportation routes, tracking information, and estimated delivery times, are produced throughout the shipping and logistics stage. BDA can analyze this data to optimize shipping routes, predict delivery times, and improve overall logistics operations for enhanced efficiency and customer satisfaction.
- *Last-mile delivery*: In some cases, RetailerX can employ various last-mile delivery options to get the package to the customer's doorstep. This includes member-exclusive ultra-fast deliveries and even innovative methods like drones in select areas. Structured data is generated during last-mile delivery, including the choice of delivery method, the assigned delivery personnel, and the actual delivery time. BDA can be utilized to track delivery performance, analyze route optimization, and identify areas for improvement in the last-mile delivery process.
- *Customer service*: Throughout the entire process, RetailerX provides proactive and responsive customer service. Customers can track their orders, get updates on delivery status, and contact customer support if needed. Semi-structured data is generated during customer service interactions, including inquiries, requests, feedback, and issue resolutions. This data encompasses customer communications, response times, satisfaction ratings, and the effectiveness of the support provided. BDA can analyze this data to identify customer service trends, improve response times, personalize customer interactions, and proactively address customer concerns.

At each stage of the customer order process, BDA can extract insights, optimize operations, enhance customer experiences, and drive continuous improvement in the SC. RetailerX can enhance its customer-centric approach, improve SC efficiency, and deliver superior customer services by analyzing and leveraging the vast amounts of data generated at each stage.

2.3.2   Big Data Life Cycle

The BD life cycle refers to the stages of collecting, managing, processing, and utilizing BD (Fig. 2.2). It encompasses the entire data lifespan, from data generation to interpretation and action. Understanding the BD life cycle is critical for CCSSC of the future as it provides a basic framework to manage and organize BD effectively. Identifying different technologies and tools associated with data generation, acquisition, storage, processing, analysis, and visualization can help organizations implement data governance, assurance, security, and management practices. Compliance and security become even more critical as modern SCs are highly interconnected and rely on cross-border transactions. BD life cycle is also essential to continuously improve the data management processes by identifying bottlenecks, inefficiencies, and scalability issues associated with various processes from data generation to interpretation and action. Based on the five Vs of BD, the requirements associated with various processes, from data generation to interpretation and action, continuously evolve with the introduction of innovative digital technologies, dynamic business models, changes to external environments, SC disruptions, risks, etc. There are several models proposed by researchers for the BD management life cycle, such as the "8 Steps Model in the Data Life Cycle" by Stobierski T. [12], the data life cycle management model [13], and the nine-stage model starting with business case evaluation [14]. The focus of this section is not comparing different BD life cycle models; rather, this section will focus on providing a comprehensive understanding of the BD life cycle process using a seven-step model.

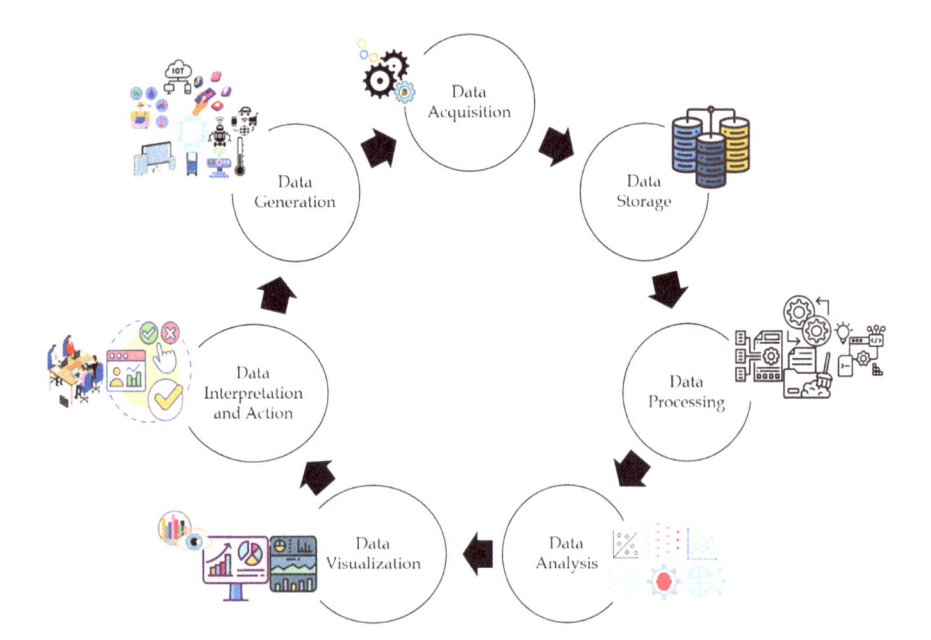

Fig. 2.2 Big data life cycle

- *Data generation*: In a SC web, a large variety of data is generated from various sources such as sensors, RFIDs, edge devices, social media, transactions, log files, and more. The data can be structured, semi-structured, or unstructured. Examples include business-to-business (B2B) and business-to-consumer (B2C) transactions (such as data related to orders, assets, geolocations, customer interactions, etc.), machine sensor readings, website clickstream data, and social media posts. Data generation is vital in SCs as it is the foundation for all subsequent activities and decision-making processes. It provides valuable insights into customer behavior, market trends, operational performance, and other critical aspects that influence the efficiency and effectiveness of SC operations. At the same time, data generation adds complexity to the BD analysis process due to the sheer volume of data generated on near real-time bases through a variety of sources. In service-based SCs, ensuring the quality and integrity of the generated data becomes crucial. Organizations need to invest in advanced technologies, data management processes, and analytical capabilities to manage the complexity of data generation in service-based SCs effectively.
- *Data acquisition*: Data acquisition is a crucial step in the BD life cycle as it enables the collection of raw data from diverse sources. It forms the foundation for subsequent stages, such as data storage, data cleansing, data integration, and data analytics, ultimately leading to valuable insights and actionable outcomes in SCM. Data acquisition methods include batch processing, real-time streaming, or data integration from external sources [15, 16]. Organizations can ensure relevant and timely data availability for further analysis and decision-making by employing appropriate data acquisition methods [16].

  - *Batch processing*: In batch processing, data is collected and processed in batches at regular intervals. This approach is suitable when the data does not require real-time analysis and can be collected periodically. For example, in a SC context, daily or hourly sales data from various retail stores can be collected and processed in batches to understand overall sales trends and inventory levels.
  - *Real-time streaming*: Real-time streaming involves collecting and processing data as it is generated in real time. This approach is suitable when immediate insights or actions are required based on up-to-date information. For instance, real-time streaming in an e-commerce SC can capture and analyze customer clickstream data to personalize product recommendations or trigger real-time inventory updates.
  - *Data integration from external sources*: Data acquisition may involve integrating data from external sources to enrich the existing datasets. For example, in a customer-centric SC, data from external sources such as social media platforms, customer review sites, or market research reports can be acquired and integrated with internal customer data to understand customer preferences and sentiments comprehensively.
  - *Sensor data collection*: In SCs that rely on IoT devices, sensors, Radio Frequency Identification (RFID), and Geo devices to capture real-time data

related to various parameters such as temperature, humidity, location, or product movement. Data acquisition in this context involves collecting and processing data from sensors installed throughout the SC network. For instance, in a cold chain logistics operation, temperature sensors in refrigerated trucks can collect data on temperature fluctuations during transportation, ensuring the quality and safety of perishable goods.

– *Other forms*: Not all data collection processes are automated. For instance, transaction-oriented systems use manual data entry to generate order, customer, or inventory information. Data can also be collected through web forms, surveys, interviews, and direct observations.

• *Data storage*: In this phase, the acquired data is stored in a suitable data storage infrastructure. Data storage plays a crucial role in the BD life cycle by providing a reliable and scalable infrastructure for storing and managing data. It enables efficient data retrieval, processing, and analysis, leading to valuable insights and informed decision-making in SCM. This may involve data warehouses, data lakes, cloud-based systems, distributed file systems, or blockchains. The choice of storage depends on data volume, velocity, variety, and specific requirements of the analytics processes to be performed.

– *Relational database*: In a SC, a relational database can store transactional structured data, such as customer information, order details, product catalogs, and inventory data.
– *Data warehouses*: Data warehouses consolidate structured and semi-structured data from multiple sources and provide a unified view of the data for reporting and analysis [13]. In a SC context, a data warehouse can store data from different systems, such as sales, inventory, and logistics, allowing for comprehensive reporting and analysis of key performance indicators.
– *Data lakes*: Data lakes are repositories that store large volumes of raw and unstructured data and provide a flexible and scalable storage solution for diverse data types [14]. In a SC, a data lake can store data from sources like customer feedback, social media posts, sensor readings, and log files. The data can be stored in its original format, enabling various data analytics and processing techniques to extract valuable insights.
– *Cloud-based storage*: Cloud storage provides on-demand capacity, eliminating the need for upfront infrastructure investments. Cloud storage is often used with other data storage technologies to store and manage large volumes of data in a distributed and accessible manner. For example, Amazon S3, Microsoft, or Google Cloud Storage offer scalable and cost-effective storage options for BD.
– *Distributed file systems*: Systems like Apache Hadoop HDFS (Hadoop Distributed File System) are designed to store and process BD across a cluster of servers. These distributed systems provide fault-tolerant and scalable storage capabilities for BD applications [17]. A distributed file system in SC analytics can store and process large volumes of data from different sources, enabling distributed processing and analysis.

- *Blockchain technology*: Blockchain is a decentralized and distributed ledger technology that allows multiple participants to provide transparency, security, and immutability for recording and verifying transactions or digital assets by maintaining and synchronizing a shared database. Blockchain technology uses cryptographic algorithms and consensus mechanisms to ensure the integrity and consensus of the shared ledger among participants [18]. It is commonly associated with applications such as cryptocurrencies, SC traceability, smart contracts, and decentralized finance. Chapters 3 and 5 discuss the blockchain technology in more detail.

  It is important to note that both distributed file systems and blockchain technologies involve distributed data storage. However, both technologies differ in their objectives and characteristics. Distributed file systems focus on storing and processing large volumes of data efficiently, while blockchain creates a decentralized and secure network for transparent and tamper-proof transactional records via distributed ledger technology. Therefore, blockchain can be utilized in SC applications to enhance transparency, traceability, and trust among SC participants by recording and validating transactions or events as immutable and auditable.

- *Data processing*: Once the data is stored, it needs to be processed and transformed into a usable format for analysis. Data processing is a crucial phase in the BD life cycle. It involves transforming raw data into a usable format for analysis and extracting valuable insight—cleaning the data, handling missing values, aggregating and summarizing data, performing data integration, and preparing it for analysis. Data processing techniques may include [19]:

  - *Data cleansing*: Data cleaning involves identifying and correcting errors, inconsistencies, and inaccuracies in the data. Data cleaning can help address duplicate customer records, missing or incorrect contact information, or inconsistent product descriptions. Organizations can make more accurate and reliable decisions based on the processed data by ensuring data quality.
  - *Data integration*: Data integration combines data from different sources or systems to create a unified and comprehensive view. For example, customer data from various touchpoints, such as online purchases, in-store transactions, customer service interactions, and social media interactions, can be merged to generate a holistic understanding of customer behavior and preferences.
  - *Data aggregation and summarization*: Aggregating and summarizing data involves condensing large volumes of data into meaningful and actionable insights. Organizations can aggregate customer data to identify trends, patterns, and customer segments. For example, data can be aggregated to understand the most popular products or services, customer purchase patterns, or seasonal variations in customer demand.
  - *Data enrichment*: Data enrichment enhances the existing data by combining it with additional information from external sources. For example, appending demographic, geographic, or social media data to customer profiles. This

enriched data provides deeper insights into customer preferences, interests, and behavior, enabling personalized and targeted service offerings.

- *Data filtering*: Data filtering involves selecting and extracting relevant data based on specific criteria or requirements. For instance, organizations can filter and select data based on customer segments, geographic regions, product categories, or time periods. This enables focused analysis and targeted decision-making to serve specific customer groups better.
- *Data normalization*: Data normalization involves transforming data into a consistent and standardized format. Data normalization can be applied to customer attributes such as names, addresses, or product descriptions to ensure uniformity and consistency. This allows for accurate analysis and comparison across different datasets.

• *Data analysis*: In this phase, the processed data is analyzed to extract meaningful insights and derive actionable conclusions. Various approaches such as descriptive (statistical, advanced visualization, dashboarding, etc.), predictive (statistical, artificial intelligence (AI)/ML, methods for forecasting/classification, etc.), prescriptive (AI/ML, optimization, etc.), and cognitive analytics (NLP) can be applied to identify patterns, correlations, trends, and anomalies within the data. The analysis results can be used to make data-driven decisions and drive business outcomes. Data analysis methods are discussed in more detail in Chap. 3.

• *Data visualization*: The insights obtained from the data analysis are visualized and presented meaningfully. This involves creating visual representations such as charts, graphs, dashboards, and reports to communicate the findings to stakeholders effectively. Data visualization helps in understanding complex patterns and trends, enabling better decision-making. Consider an e-commerce company that wants to improve its order fulfillment process. By analyzing customer data, they identify that delivery time significantly impacts customer satisfaction. To communicate this insight effectively, they create data visualization using a bar chart comparing delivery times for different regions. Through visualization, the company can show variations in delivery performance across regions, allowing them to focus on areas where improvement is needed. This visualization can be shared with the logistics team and used to drive discussions on strategies to optimize delivery processes and enhance customer satisfaction.

• *Data interpretation and action*: In this final phase, the results of the data analysis are interpreted, and appropriate actions are taken based on the insights gained. This can involve making strategic business decisions, optimizing processes, improving customer experiences, launching targeted marketing campaigns, or implementing operational changes. For example, an online streaming service organization can analyze customer data to improve its content recommendation algorithm. By analyzing user viewing patterns, preferences, and feedback, they identify that customers who watch a particular genre of movies are more likely to engage with specific TV shows. Based on this insight, the streaming service can enhance its recommendation engine to suggest relevant TV shows to customers who have shown interest in that genre. This personalized recommendation leads to increased customer satisfaction, longer engagement with the platform, and improved customer retention.

2.3.3 Big Data Ecosystem for Customer-Centric Service-Based Supply Chains of the Future

The BD ecosystem refers to the collection of technologies, tools, and frameworks used to store, process, analyze, and manage large volumes of data. It encompasses various components that work together to handle the challenges associated with BD [20]. The BD ecosystem is critical to support data-driven decisions, product/service personalization and customization, SC optimization, and enhancing customers' overall experience. This can help organizations align their SC strategies with their customers' value chain activities and unique needs, increasing customer satisfaction, loyalty, and business success. In order to capture value, the BD ecosystem involves various actors, from data generators to technology providers and information and knowledge consumers.

- *Data providers*: These are CPS entities that generate or provide the raw data, such as individuals, organizations, sensors, devices, social media platforms, websites, and more. Data providers may offer structured, semi-structured, or unstructured data.
- *Data consumers*: Data is consumed by various CPS entities, such as businesses, organizations, researchers, analysts, data scientists, end users, and automated systems (chatbots, autonomous decision-making systems), to make data-driven informed decisions.
- *Data aggregators*: These are the entities that collect and aggregate data from multiple sources to generate value for specific needs. They may specialize in consolidating data from various providers organizing and preparing it for further processing and analysis. For example, Bloomberg[1] aggregates and analyzes data from various financial markets, news sources, and company reports to provide real-time financial information, market analysis, and trading tools to financial professionals. Similarly, Dun & Bradstreet[2] aggregates and curates business-related data from various sources, including public records, financial statements, industry reports, and their proprietary data sources. Businesses use their data for market research, risk assessment, lead generation, and supplier evaluation.
- *Data processors*: These entities process and analyze the data to extract meaningful insights and patterns. Data processors can be data scientists, analysts, or specialized data analytics firms. They employ various techniques and technologies, such as ML, statistical analysis, and data mining, to extract valuable information from the data.

---

[1] https://www.bloomberg.com/canada

[2] https://www.dnb.com/ca-en/

- *Data storage and infrastructure providers*: These entities provide the infrastructure and technologies to store, manage, and process BD. They may offer cloud-based storage solutions, distributed file systems, databases, blockchain, and computing resources required to handle large volumes of data. Some of the major providers include IBM Cloud, Oracle Cloud, Microsoft Azure, and AWS, to name a few.
- *Data governance and security providers*: These entities ensure data privacy, security, compliance, and ethical use of data. They may provide tools, technologies, and services to manage data governance, data quality, access controls, and data protection measures. IBM Cloud Pak for Data, SAP Master Data Governance, and Alation Data Governance App are among the service providers.
- *Data visualization and reporting providers*: These entities specialize in visualizing and presenting data meaningfully and interactively. They offer tools and platforms for creating charts, graphs, dashboards, and reports that facilitate data-driven decision-making and enhance understanding of complex datasets. Microsoft Power BI, Looker, Tableau, and Domo provide data visualization software and platforms.
- *Data application developers*: These entities develop applications, software, and systems that leverage BD. They create solutions that enable data-driven insights, automate processes, and deliver value to end users. These applications span various domains, such as CRM, SC optimization, fraud detection, and predictive analytics.

In summary, the BD ecosystem empowers businesses to gather, analyze, and act upon customer data in real time. This data-driven approach enables businesses to understand customers better, anticipate their needs, personalize interactions, optimize SC operations, and ultimately deliver exceptional customer-centric experiences.

2.4   Data-Driven Customer-Centric Service-Based Supply Chains: Industry Example and Insights

Upon learning about technology and automation in the workplace, people often become concerned about job security. Starbucks CEO Kevin Johnson aims to alter this perception by utilizing digital tools to enhance the human experience and cultivate stronger relationships between employees and customers. To accomplish this objective, Starbucks employs its internal AI platform, Deep Brew, to enhance various aspects of the company's operations, including SCM and customer-centric initiatives [21]. This section explores three essential avenues contributing to Starbucks' success in leveraging data: fostering customer loyalty, empowering frontline workers, and strengthening SC connections.

2.4.1 Fostering Customer Loyalty

By leveraging data analysis and AI algorithms, Starbucks has evolved its approach from analyzing data for all stores to understanding the unique characteristics of each location. This shift allows them to offer personalized recommendations and promotions tailored to individual stores. AI-driven personalization encompasses thoughtful choices based on local store inventory, popular selections, weather conditions, time of day, community preferences, and previous orders. For instance, Starbucks strategically introduced "Starbucks Evenings[3]"at select locations based on data indicating high alcohol consumption in those areas. They also use data to create special limited-offering menu items that align with current trends or events. For example, during a heatwave in Memphis, Tennessee, Starbucks launched a local Frappuccino promotion to attract customers to cool down [22]. Despite having countless beverage combinations, Starbucks continuously monitors data to identify best-selling drinks and adapts its menu based on local tastes. Starbucks' success in providing data-driven customer-centric service is evident through the exceptional personalized customer experience, which caters to each customer's unique preferences and needs.

2.4.2 Empowering Frontline Workers

Data-driven insights play a crucial role in guiding Starbucks' strategic decisions, from optimizing scheduling to refining product offerings. The company's vision of AI is not to replace humans but to act as an invisible sidekick, automating tasks such as inventory management and equipment maintenance prediction. Although customers may not directly perceive the automation, they benefit from a more efficient and personalized experience when baristas' time is freed up. One remarkable application of AI at Starbucks is its real-time response to customer demands. By analyzing customer data and order patterns, AI streamlines beverage preparation, ensuring timely order fulfillment. For instance, if a customer places a mobile order for iced lattes but is still a distance away from the store, AI prompts baristas to prioritize other beverages, guaranteeing optimal drink quality upon the customer's arrival [21]. The company's commitment to using AI as an enabling technology rather than a human replacement exemplifies its dedication to delivering outstanding customer-centric service.

---

[3] https://stories.starbucks.com/stories/2015/starbucks-evenings-stores/

2.4.3 Strengthening Supply Chain Connections

Starbucks embraces BD to connect its entire SC, enhancing transparency and traceability. Their "bean to cup" pilot utilizes blockchain technology and allows customers to scan coffee bags and trace the origins of beans, creating a one-to-one connection between coffee farmers and coffee enthusiasts worldwide [23]. In partnership with Conservation International, Starbucks actively gathers critical feedback from coffee suppliers to foster sustainable coffee production [24]. Integrating BD and blockchain strengthens Starbucks' relationship with customers, enabling them to connect with the people and regions behind their favorite coffee blends. This commitment to traceability and sustainability reflects Starbucks' core values, ensuring that every cup of coffee served is not only delightful but also ethically sourced, supporting communities and promoting environmental conservation.

In summary, Starbucks embraces a data-driven, customer-centric SC by leveraging AI to optimize operations, enhance the customer experience, and empower employees to deliver highly personalized service. By using data-driven insights, Starbucks aims to create a seamless and tailored journey for customers while maintaining the human touch that defines its brand.

2.5 Analysis of the Impact of Big Data Analytics on Supply Chains

As discussed in Chap. 1, CCSSCs require integration, seamless interaction, and coordination between SC partners spanning from lower-tier suppliers to end-consumers. The power of BDA can play a key role in enabling these conditions and providing tailored, agile, trustworthy, and innovative services.

The usage of IoT devices and extended ICT infrastructures within SCs can generate large volumes of data in real time. Concurrently, the advancements in relational database technologies (database management systems (DBMS), data warehouses, data marts, online analytical processing (OLAP), etc.) allow gathering, manipulation, and querying through datasets to obtain new insights [25]. These capabilities can significantly enhance SCM and customer-centricity. Following are some examples of how the amalgamation of BD generation, database technologies, and analytical capabilities can positively impact different areas of SCM.

2.5.1 Supply Chain Risk Management

Monitoring real-time data can improve the transparency, traceability, and reliability of logistics operations by mapping the real world into the virtual world [25]. BDA-based intelligent transport systems allow traffic flow prediction, real-time safety monitoring of expressway traffic, and efficient vehicle path planning [26]. The connectedness through IoT can result in a more system-oriented approach toward remote monitoring and a better alignment of the physical world and computer-based systems. The application of analytical models can enable decision-makers to transform data into predictions and prescriptions for structural improvements through a system-oriented approach. For example, intelligent data analytics may stimulate organizations to act more resiliently and proactively in real time once a disturbance is observed or predicted [25, 27]. BDA brings a new source of competitive advantages for logistics service providers and users to carry out SCM so as to obtain the ability to adjust under demand and capacity fluctuations on a real-time basis [28]. Sensors and other data sources can be used to evaluate the delivery performance of vendors, forecast vendors' likelihood of achieving the required performance under disruptions, and select vendors or renew contracts based on performance [29].

Cisco Systems has been ranked the top global SC by Gartner for three consecutive years (2020–22). The key factor in Cisco's top spot in Gartner's Global SC 25 is its adaptability to deal with the changing environment through realignments [30]. Cisco's SCRM is based on pairing risk intelligence (knowing where the vulnerabilities are) with risk analytics (finding where the highest probabilities for the disruptions are). Their key tools for risk intelligence and analytics include business continuity planning and visualization, which comprehensively capture the SC web and build resilience capabilities deeper into the supplier sub-tiers [31]. The planning part collects information on key suppliers and nodes in the SC on a continuous basis. The visualization part provides a capability to quickly assess the impact of an event by identifying which SC nodes are in the affected region, what parts or products are made there, and what alternate sites can be engaged. This visualization and the underlying data become the starting point for any incident mitigation effort. This allows Cisco to quantify the potential impact of an incident on its SC operations.

Blockchain technology, which can produce and secure high-quality BD, is also making a mark on traceability and risk management in SCs [32]. The blockchain technology, in the context of Service 4.0, is discussed further in chapters 3 and 5.

2.5.2 Product Servicing

The availability of high-volume real-time data through IoT and BDA can also enable Smart Product Service Systems (SPSS), allowing efficient service-oriented and digitalized value propositions [27]. SPSS refers to a system based on networked smart products and service systems for providing new functionalities leveraging digital architectures, IoT, cloud computing, and analytics. Typical examples are remote product monitoring, remote diagnostics, predictive maintenance, and optimization of equipment based on operational data [33]. The accumulation and analysis of massive data about various individual and industrial activities enables the encapsulation of manufacturing resources to form on-demand tailored services for customers. Thanks to the combination of sensors and cloud computing, products can be remotely monitored to provide data about product usage, which is required for service processing. Moreover, the use of AI can provide richer and more reliable data and analytics for decision-making in predictive maintenance. SPSS helps create a stronger long-term client relationship based on end value for the client and is a way to differentiate in the market [27]. Intelligent immersive system [34], a mixed-reality-based service operations framework that is closely related to SPSS, proposes a feedback loop between the client and service provider for continuous knowledge and service enhancement (Fig. 2.3).

2.5.3 Quality Management and Operational Efficiency

In the quality management domain, tracing, monitoring, and BDA can help companies generate and exploit data-centric insights to define and implement timely corrective actions. Rooted in blockchain technology, which can produce and secure high-quality BD [32], Walmart can trace a specific package of fresh food items to its source in less than three seconds as opposed to several days [35]. This capability can revolutionize food safety and quality management, which has been a major challenge in global food SCs.

Digitization and BDA provide a major opportunity for producers to manage operations efficiently in general by improving productivity, quality, and waste reduction [26, 27]. Many world-class business organizations, including pharmaceutical, garments, automotive, retail, healthcare, and financial services, use BDA tools to minimize processing flaws, increase efficiency, increase productivity, improve production quality, and save time and money [33]. The following are some examples. Merck, a pharmaceutical firm specializing in producing vaccines, uses the BDA to optimize its manufacturing. Raytheon Corp. has used BD to enable smart

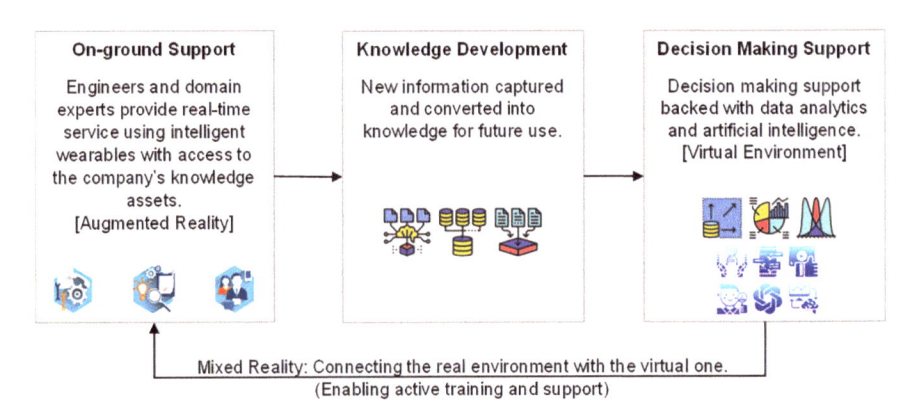

Fig. 2.3 Intelligent immersive systems for service operations

factories, which are based on the powerful capacity to manage information from various data sources such as Computer-Aided Design (CAD) models, sensors, instruments, Internet transactions, simulations, and digital records in the company. Itron, a water meter manufacturer, uses BDA to provide "smart grid" solutions, supporting the analysis of consumption patterns and habits, and leak detections remotely, as a superior service to which its customers are locked in. Schmitz Cargobull, a German truck body and trailer maker, uses telecommunications and data to supervise the maintenance, cargo temperatures, and routes by its trailers. Toyota Motor carried out a BD-based live traffic service using 700,000 of its vehicles on roads. The service, targeting local governments and businesses, has the potential to earn billions of USD for Toyota. Siemens, using thousands of daily measurements from its power plants around the world, developed a remote diagnostic service for operational analysis. Rolls-Royce uses BD from sensors on different engine components and systems in the field to improve product quality [28]. Connectivity and real-time data gathering can reveal the location and status of assets, maintenance requirements, stock positioning to control service levels, and the relationship between shipment types and delivery performance for improving operational and supply chain efficiency [29].

2.5.4 Consumer Behavior

Overall, BD technologies have connected SC echelons to streamline communication with one another to create intelligent SCs. At the consumer level as well, a profusion of connected devices has enabled more active customer engagement. At the downstream, advanced Point-of-Sale (POS) systems, IoT, and user-generated online content provide vast amounts of data and a rich opportunity to understand consumer behavior, improve demand predictions, and devise appropriate pricing policies [37]. Processing consumer data from websites can enable more personalized product offerings, increasing the chance of purchases and customer retention [28, 29]. The analysis of downstream data can help to plan and execute the entire SC more effectively and efficiently.

Traffic data, which has become much easier for retailers to gather in recent years, can provide key insights into consumer behavior and the decision-making process. When combined with sales data, the potential of traffic data increases significantly. The combination can reveal trends in conversion (i.e., visit-to-purchase ratio), which in turn can inform about the effectiveness of different in-store strategies. Adding the data on the consumer's behavior prior to store (online or physical) visit adds yet another layer of useful insights. The prior consumer activities can indicate purchasing intent and improve the forecasting process. The explosion of online activities over the last decade has made it easier to obtain data that was previously hard to get [37].

2.5.5 Impact on the Triple Bottom Line

Even as many BD technologies are in their infancy, the positive impact of BDA on the financial, social, and environmental performance of the SC is evident. Examples show BDA can impact all three aspects of sustainability. For example, a reduction in transportation distance and delays through BDA-based smarter logistics planning can lead to lower costs and emissions. BDA-centered humanitarian SC can enable trust, flexibility, collaboration, and control in humanitarian efforts [26]. Data collection and analysis are helping apparel companies to track the environmental impact of their products in a precise and transparent way [38], precious stone companies with unprecedented traceability to avoid conflict diamonds [35], and food companies, like Nestle, to monitor and control deforestation [39].

2.6 Big Data Implementation Challenges for Customer-Centric Service-Based Supply Chains

Although BDA can revolutionize SCM, its implementation poses significant challenges. The BDA adoption examples stated in the previous section are limited and do not represent the state of BDA use in general. The SCM literature, in most cases, has only suggested BDA frameworks in SCM [26], while the number of validated implementations of these frameworks remains limited [25]. Many companies focus on large-scale data collection but cannot drive decisions based on the data [28].

Several constraints impede the wider adoption of BDA across industries, regions, and SC segments. According to the SCM BDA frameworks, the data collection and processing requires the adoption and proliferation of IoT devices. However, core and resource-intensive SCM activities—transportation and warehousing—are largely based on physical assets empowered by primitive or no data handling capabilities. At the same time, the IoT paradigm has not fully matured [25]. This casts doubt on the possibility and mechanics of the use of IoT data in decision-making, at least in the near future. Regarding the BDA tools, as true for analytical modeling in general, incorporating the data source's uncertainty is required for the sound representation of the problem context and the model and analysis validity. However, capturing uncertainty can significantly impact the simplicity of the tools used by decision-makers, exposing a trade-off between validity and adaptability. BDA models and tools are inherently more complex due to the scale and complexity of this input and the requirement of the integration of various data sources.

Besides the complexities of BDA systems, another major barrier to BDA adoption is the cost. Empowering current SC assets or acquiring new equipment for data generation and transmission through IoT can be expensive. Implementing, maintaining, and running these systems also require highly skilled professionals who can be difficult and expensive to hire due to the high overall demand for their skills in the wider tech industry. The resourceful companies may be able to overcome the cost barriers, but smaller players in the SCs can lag behind. Small and medium-sized enterprises (SMEs) in Europe, despite being linked to 85% of employment, struggle to create value through SPSS offerings [27]. The lack of the implementation of data capturing and transmission systems in parts of SCs can fail the overarching connectivity required in CCSSC from lower-tier suppliers to consumers. The poor IT infrastructure, e.g., legacy Internet technologies, in several developing and underdeveloped countries, can also create a bottleneck in achieving overall connectivity and integration [26, 36, 37]. Other examples of challenges that can be observed in the implementation of blockchain technology are discussed in Sect. 2.4. Implementing blockchain requires all SC partners to have a mature platform with credible architecture and strong internal knowledge [27]. These conditions could be challenging even for one product. The complexity can increase manyfold if the product mix and sources are large. Integration remains a challenge in conventional SCs. In CCSSCs, which focus on personalized services, real-time responsiveness, and seamless experience for consumers with multiple purchase channels, downstream management and integration can add to the overall SC integration challenges.

The most highlighted issues in BDA implementation relate to data security and privacy. Connected devices and sensors can constantly collect large amounts of sensitive customer data without anonymization. This can result in identity theft during transmission or even from storage devices. Several incidents of data breaches have resulted in millions of customer data records being compromised. Another data-related concern is the bias in data [37]. For example, how data is collected can result in discrimination of certain customer segments based on demographics.

References

1. McKinsey & Company. (2015). *Marketing & sales - big data, analytics, and the future of marketing & sales*. McKinsey & Company Report. Retrieved May 9, 2023, from https://www. mckinsey.com/~/media/McKinsey/Business%20Functions/Marketing%20and%20Sales/ Our%20Insights/EBook%20Big%20data%20analytics%20and%20the%20future%20of%20 marketing%20sales/Big-Data-eBook.ashx
2. Gartner IT Glossary. (2012). Definition of big data. Retrieved May 9, 2023, from https://www. gartner.com/it-glossary/big-data/
3. Perry, J. S. (2017). What is big data? More than volume, velocity and variety. IBM Developer Report. Retrieved May 9, 2023, from https://developer.ibm.com/blogs/ what-is-big-data-more-than-volume-velocity-and-variety/
4. Yonus, M. (2019). Research challenges of big data. *Service Oriented Computing and Applications, 13*, 105–107. https://doi.org/10.1007/s11761-019-00265-x
5. International Roadmap for Devices and Systems (IRDS). (2016). IEEE advanced technology for humans - Factory integration white paper. Retrieved May 9, 2023, from https://irds.ieee. org/images/files/pdf/2016_FI.pdf
6. Witkowski, K. (2017). Internet of things, big data, industry 4.0–innovative solutions in logistics and supply chains management. *Procedia Engineering, 182*, 763–769. https://doi. org/10.1016/j.proeng.2017.03.197

7. ProjectPro. (2023). How big data analysis helped increase Walmart's sales turnover? Retrieved May 9, 2023, from https://www.projectpro.io/article/how-big-data-analysis-helped-increase-walmarts-sales-turnover/109

8. Statista. (2022). Number of Internet of Things (IoT) connected devices worldwide from 2019 to 2021, with forecasts from 2022 to 2030. Retrieved May 9, 2023, from https://www.statista.com/statistics/1183457/iot-connected-devices-worldwide/#:~:text=Number%20of%20IoT%20connected%20devices,2021%2C%20with%20forecasts%20to%202030&text=The%20number%20of%20Internet%20of,billion%20IoT%20devices%20in%202030

9. Statista. (2021). Volume of data/information created, captured, copied, and consumed worldwide from 2010 to 2020, with forecasts from 2021 to 2025. Retrieved May 9, 2023, from https://www.statista.com/statistics/871513/worldwide-data-created/#:~:text=The%20total%20amount%20of%20data,to%20more%20than%20180%20zettabytes

10. Gandomi, A., & Haider, M. (2015). Beyond the hype: Big data concepts, methods, and analytics. *International Journal of Information Management, 35*(2), 137–144. https://doi.org/10.1016/j.ijinfomgt.2014.10.007

11. Büyüközkan, G., & Göçer, F. (2018). Digital supply chain: Literature review and a proposed framework for future research. *Computers in Industry, 97*(4), 157–177. https://doi.org/10.1016/j.compind.2018.02.010

12. Stobierski, T. (2021). *8 steps in the data life cycle*. Harvard Business School Online. Retrieved May 9, 2023, from https://online.hbs.edu/blog/post/data-life-cycle

13. IBM. What is a data warehouse? Retrieved May 9, 2023, from https://www.ibm.com/topics/data-warehouse

14. IBM. What is a data lake? Retrieved May 9, 2023, from https://www.ibm.com/topics/data-lake

15. IBM Topics. (n.d.). ETL (Extract, Transform, Load). Retrieved July 15, 2023, from https://www.ibm.com/topics/etl

16. Lyko, K., Nitzschke, M., & Ngomo, A. N. (2016). *Big data acquisition. New horizons for a data-driven economy: A roadmap for usage and exploitation of big data in Europe* (pp. 39–62). Springer Open.

17. DataBricks. Hadoop distributed file system (HDFS). Retrieved May 9, 2023, from https://www.databricks.com/glossary/hadoop-distributed-file-system-hdfs

18. IBM. What is blockchain technology? Retrieved May 9, 2023, from https://www.ibm.com/topics/blockchain

19. Oussous, A., Benjelloun, F. Z., Lahcen, A., & A., & Belfkih, S. (2018). Big data technologies: A survey. *Journal of King Saud University-Computer and Information Sciences, 30*(4), 431–448. https://doi.org/10.1016/j.jksuci.2017.06.001

20. Anwar, M. J., Gill, A. Q., Hussain, F. K., & Imran, M. (2021). Secure big data ecosystem architecture: Challenges and solutions. *EURASIP Journal on Wireless and Communications and Networking, 1*, 1–30. https://doi.org/10.1186/s13638-021-01996-2

21. Warnick, J. (2020, January 10). *AI for humanity: How Starbucks plans to use technology to nurture the human spirit*. Starbucks Stories & News. Retrieved June 27, 2023, from https://stories.starbucks.com/stories/2020/how-starbucks-plans-to-use-technology-to-nurture-the-human-spirit/

22. Marr, B. (2018, May 28). *Starbucks: Using big data, analytics and artificial intelligence to boost performance*. Forbes. Retrieved June 27, 2023, from https://www.forbes.com/sites/bernardmarr/2018/05/28/starbucks-using-big-data-analytics-and-artificial-intelligence-to-boost-performance/?sh=571138d065cd

23. Starbucks. (2018, March 21). *Starbucks to pilot 'bean to cup' traceability with new technology*. Starbucks Stories & News. Retrieved June 27, 2023, from https://stories.starbucks.com/stories/2018/starbucks-to-pilot-bean-to-cup-traceability/

24. Warnick, J. (2020, September 29). *New StarbucksTraceability tool explores bean-to-cup journey*. Starbucks Stories Canada. Retrieved June 27, 2023, from https://stories.starbucks.ca/en-ca/stories/2020/new-starbucks-traceability-tool-explores-bean-to-cup-journey/

25. Koot, M., Mes, M. R., & Iacob, M. E. (2021). A systematic literature review of supply chain decision making supported by the internet of things and big data analytics. *Computers & Industrial Engineering, 154*, 1–28. https://doi.org/10.1016/j.cie.2020.107076

26. Raut, R. D., Mangla, S. K., Narwane, V. S., Dora, M., & Liu, M. (2021). Big data analytics as a mediator in lean, agile, resilient, and green (LARG) practices effects on sustainable supply chains. *Transportation Research Part E: Logistics and Transportation Review, 145*(1), 102170. https://doi.org/10.1016/j.tre.2020.102170

27. Le-Dain, M. A., Benhayoun, L., Matthews, J., & Liard, M. (2023). Barriers and opportunities of digital servitization for SMEs: The effect of smart product-service system business models. *Service Business, 17*(1), 359–393.

28. Zhong, R. Y., Newman, S. T., Huang, G. Q., & Lan, S. (2016). Big data for supply chain management in the service and manufacturing sectors: Challenges, opportunities, and future perspectives. *Computers & Industrial Engineering, 101*, 572–591. https://doi.org/10.1016/j.cie.2016.07.013

29. DHL. Big data analytics: Relevance to the future of logistics. Retrieved November 08, 2023, from https://www.dhl.com/global-en/home/insights-and-innovation/thought-leadership/trend-reports/big-data-analytics.html

30. Stamford, C. (2022, May 26) Gartner. Gartner announces rankings of the 2022 Global Supply Chain Top 25. Retrieved June 27, 2023, from https://www.gartner.com/en/newsroom/press-releases/2022-05-26-gartner-announces-rankings-of-the-2022-global-supply-chain-top-25#:~:text=Cisco%20Systems%20scored%20the%20top,%3A%20Microsoft%2C%20Siemens%20and%20AstraZeneca

31. US Resilience Project. (2011). De-risking the supply chain: Cisco's risk intelligence and analytic tools. Retrieved June 27, 2023, from https://usresilienceproject.org/wp-content/uploads/2014/09/pdf-USRP_Cisco_CS_022912.pdf

32. Deepa, N., Pham, Q. V., Nguyen, D. C., Bhattacharya, S., Prabadevi, B., Gadekallu, T. R., Maddikunta, P. K. R., Fang, F., & Pathirana, P. N. (2022). A survey on blockchain for big data: Approaches, opportunities, and future directions. *Future Generation Computer Systems, 131*, 209–226. https://doi.org/10.1016/j.future.2022.01.017

33. Pirola, F., Boucher, X., Wiesner, S., & Pezzotta, G. (2020). Digital technologies in product-service systems: A literature review and a research agenda. *Computers in Industry, 123*, 103301. https://doi.org/10.1016/j.compind.2020.103301

34. Pena-Rios, A., Hagras, H., Owusu, G., & Gardner, M. (2018). Furthering service 4.0: Harnessing intelligent immersive environments and systems. *IEEE Systems, Man, and Cybernetics Magazine, 4*(1), 20–31.

35. Sristy, A. (2021, November 30). *Blockchain in the food supply chain - What does the Future Look Like?* Walmart Global Tech. Retrieved June 27, 2023, from https://tech.walmart.com/content/walmart-global-tech/en_us/news/articles/blockchain-in-the-food-supply-chain.html

36. Moktadir, M. A., Ali, S. M., Paul, S. K., & Shukla, N. (2019). Barriers to big data analytics in manufacturing supply chains: A case study from Bangladesh. *Computers & Industrial Engineering, 128*, 1063–1075. https://doi.org/10.1109/MSMC.2017.2769199

37. Boone, T., Ganeshan, R., Jain, A., & Sanders, N. R. (2019). Forecasting sales in the supply chain: Consumer analytics in the big data era. *International Journal of Forecasting, 35*(1), 170–180. https://doi.org/10.1016/j.ijforecast.2018.09.003

38. Sheep Inc. How the Higg Index is Heroing Plastic and Condemning Natural Fibers. Retrieved Junc 27, 2023, from https://sheepinc.com/pages/higgindex

39. Nestle. Nestlé accelerates no deforestation commitment by implementing 100% satellite monitoring coverage of its global palm oil supply chains. Retrieved June 27, 2023, from https://www.nestle.com/media/pressreleases/allpressreleases/no-deforestation-satellite-monitoring-coverage-palm-oil-supply-chains

Chapter 3
Analytics Models for Customer-Centric Service-Based Supply Chains

3.1 Introduction to Analytical Models in Supply Chain Management

Supply chain management (SCM) is an intricate orchestration of a complex and interdependent network of organizations, serving as a linchpin in the machinery of modern businesses. Its significance lies in the imperative need for effective and efficient coordination and optimization of diverse entities, processes, and resources—from raw material sourcing to the ultimate delivery of finished products and managing reverse logistics to discerning customers [1]. In the contemporary landscape, increased data availability and computational advancements have birthed a transformative era. Analytical models emerge as potent instruments, wielding the power to furnish data-driven insights that elevate the effectiveness, efficiency, and customer-centricity of SCs [1, 2]. These analytical models are not mere luxuries; they have become indispensable tools for proactive planning, shifting the paradigm from reactive responses to proactive strategies in confronting the myriad challenges within the SC.

Advanced analytics models empower organizations to identify historical inefficiencies, foresee demand undulations and potential SC risks, and proffer alternative courses of action to manage and mitigate these fluctuations. This proactive stance enables the alignment of SC strategies with overarching business objectives and the ever-evolving demands of the customer. In an era awash with data, the utilization of analytical models ceases to be a mere option; it is imperative for SC professionals aspiring to optimize operations and maintain competitiveness in the dynamic crucible of contemporary markets.

This chapter aims to delve into a comprehensive understanding of four pivotal analytical models—descriptive analytics, predictive analytics, prescriptive analytics, and cognitive analytics—and their profound applications in the realm of SCM. Through this exploration, the chapter unravels the transformative potential

P. S. Kang et al., *Service 4.0*, SpringerBriefs in Service Science, https://doi.org/10.1007/978-3-031-63875-6_3

these models hold, steering the course toward a future where SCs are not just managed but optimized with acumen and foresight. Chapter 4 will use a case-based approach to exemplify the application of analytical models.

3.2 Different Types of Analytics Models

3.2.1 Descriptive Analytics for Understanding Past and Current Supply Chain Performance

Descriptive analytics is the fundamental and widely used approach in data analysis for summarizing historical patterns and answering the question, "What happened" or "What is happening" [3]? Companies often gather vast amounts of data, but the data's significance remains obscured without meaningful descriptions. For instance, a retail giant (such as Walmart) may be keen on optimizing its sales performance. For Walmart, analysis of data collected from millions of sales globally can provide valuable insights. Through the lens of descriptive analytics, the retail organization can discern patterns in customer purchasing behavior, identify the best-selling products, and unveil geographical regions exhibiting notable sales growth or decline. The organization can create concise summaries that paint a vivid picture of its historical performance by extracting relevant information from the data. This, in turn, empowers decision-makers to understand their market dynamics, identify successful strategies, and pinpoint areas for improvement.

More specifically, summarization reports and visualizations, such as pie charts, bar charts, and interactive tables within dashboards (Fig. 3.1), are common tools for descriptive analytics. For example, understanding average revenue per customer enables an online shopping company to assess its current business performance across different departments. Identifying the primary supplier helps a manufacturing company refine its SC strategy.

Sometimes treated as a separate analytics stream, diagnostic analytics takes one step further and requires more drilled-down and data mining abilities to answer the question, "Why did it happen"? It is also called root cause analysis and is grouped into the descriptive analytics category in existing literature [5–7]. Consider a hypothetical scenario within a retail organization's logistics department. Descriptive analytics, for example, can shed light on an overall increase in transportation costs for the latest quarter. However, this broad insight only scratches the surface. The logistics team embarks on diagnostic analytics to identify the underlying factors contributing to this cost escalation, akin to a detective meticulously examining clues.

In this case, the analytics team may perform a variance analysis by region, investigating the freight costs between warehouses. Consider that the analysis unveils a glaring anomaly—a higher-than-expected cost for shipments within a specific region. This revelation serves as the starting point for a deeper investigation, reminiscent of a detective uncovering the layers of a complex case. As the logistics team

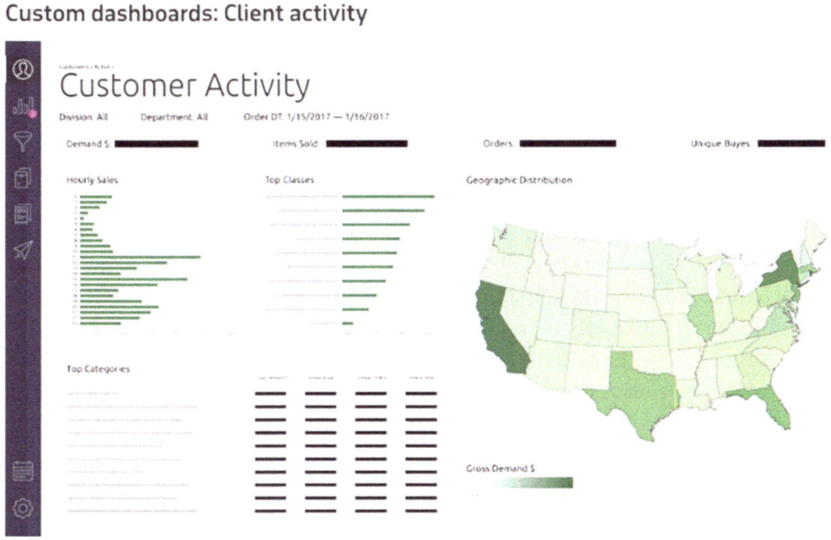

Custom dashboards: Client activity

Fig. 3.1 Sample dashboard of descriptive analytics solution [4]

delves further, they may discover that inaccurate sales forecasts for products in that region have led to severe stockouts. Consequently, the organization has been compelled to expedite shipments to meet demand, incurring additional transportation costs. The root cause analysis, within the realm of diagnostic analytics, unveils a chain of events—imprecise sales forecasts triggering stockouts, which drive up transportation expenses.

Descriptive analytics provides essential insights into business performance and why it differs from expectations. Once patterns and issues are identified, companies can employ advanced analytics to predict outcomes, make data-driven decisions, and improve overall performance.

3.2.2 Predictive Analytics for Forecasting Future Demand and Customer Behavior

Predictive analytics emerges as a subset of advanced analytics that involves using historical and current data, along with various statistical and machine learning (ML) techniques, to predict the likely future state of the world through a deeper understanding of the relationships between inputs, constraints, and outcomes. Organizations can leverage predictive analytics to identify patterns, relationships, and potential opportunities and risks within data to aid in informed decision-making for future events. For example, companies like Uber and Amazon use predictive analytics to improve overall SC performance through accurate forecasting.

For companies like Uber, data from drivers, passengers, traffic patterns, events happening in a particular area, and weather conditions can be analyzed to predict the riders at a particular time in specific areas [8]. This can help strategically deploy drivers to meet the demand. Similarly, retail sector organizations like Walmart and Amazon utilize predictive analytics to manage their vast network of suppliers and fulfillment centers to ensure on-time delivery of orders. This entails analysis of historical demand data to understand seasonality, trend, and customer purchasing patterns combined with external real-time data from external sources such as social media, weather, web traffic, and other sources to gain a more comprehensive and nuanced understanding of customer behavior, potential SC bottlenecks and disruptions, and market trends. By incorporating these internal and external data sources in predictive analytics, organizations can optimize their SCs and internal operations and personalize customer experiences by enhancing the accuracy of predictive models [9, 10]. More specifically, predictive modeling leads to the following:

- *Improved customer experience*: Understanding customer preferences from past purchase history, clickstream data, spend analysis, etc., can help anticipate customer needs.
- *Optimal resource allocation*: Resources such as inventories (Amazon/Walmart) and assets (Uber, drivers) can be allocated efficiently to manage high-demand areas. From an inventory optimization perspective, retailers can predict demand for the most popular toys, electronics, and other gift items during the holiday season or special events (Mother's Day, Valentine's Day, back-to-school events,[1] etc.) to minimize the risks of stockouts. This proactive approach aims to minimize the potential risks of stockouts, ultimately contributing to elevated customer satisfaction and ensuring swift, reliable deliveries. Predictive analytics, in this context, serves as a valuable tool to forecast demand both in terms of location and time.
- *Cost reduction*: Optimal inventory and asset allocation lead to SC process optimization. Organizations can reduce costs by reducing unnecessary inventories, operational expenses, and inefficiencies.
- *Competitive advantage*: Organizations can leverage predictive analytics to promote data-driven decision-making for better services, shorter delivery times, and higher customer satisfaction.

---

[1] https://www.walmart.ca/cp/browse/gifts-holidays/back-to-school/6000188914393-6000197172389.

3.2.3 Prescriptive Analytics for Optimizing Supply Chain Decisions

In the context of SCM, prescriptive analytics emerges as a powerful tool, offering the ability to identify optimal solutions or courses of action to address challenges and enhance overall performance, encompassing socio-environmental considerations. This analytical branch plays a pivotal role in instilling efficiency across diverse facets of SCM, spanning inventory management, transportation, distribution, and customer relations. It builds on descriptive and predictive analysis to determine what should happen rather than what has happened (describing) and what can happen (predicting) [11]. The prescriptive branch of analytics includes various modeling approaches, such as mathematical (constraint) optimization programming, game theory, ML, and simulation.

For instance, in the context of inventory management, prescriptive analytics can guide decisions on how much inventory to hold and space to allocate for each stock-keeping unit (SKU). It can strategically advise on facility locations and the placement of inventory within the network to balance costs and responsiveness. Additionally, prescriptive analytics can influence transportation decisions, determining fleet sizes and transportation routes to minimize costs and maximize capacity utilization. Consider a scenario where prescriptive analytics is employed to fine-tune after-sales services. The system could suggest optimal service parts inventory levels by factoring in demand behavior and obsolescence risk, ensuring a balance between efficient service provision and cost.

In essence, prescriptive analytics acts as a compass for decision-makers, guiding them through the complexities of SC intricacies. By offering concrete recommendations on inventory allocation, facility locations, transportation strategies, and workforce management, it serves as a linchpin for not only achieving operational excellence but also aligning SC practices with broader business objectives.

3.2.4 Cognitive Analytics and Large Language Models for Extracting Insights from Unstructured Data and Enabling Automated Decision-Making

Cognitive analytics is an advanced form of data analysis that combines artificial intelligence (AI), ML, natural language processing (NLP), and other cognitive technologies to understand, interpret, and extract insights from unstructured data sources, such as text, images, audio, and video [12, 13]. Unlike conventional analytics, which focuses on structured data, cognitive analytics deals with the complexities of understanding human language and context, enabling systems to "think" and "reason" like humans by automating the knowledge-intensive processes through AI,

ML, NLP, and other techniques. Large language models (LLM), such as chatGPT,[2] bidirectional encoder representations from transformers (BERT[3]), Claude,[4] JenniAi,[5] etc., are closely linked to cognitive analytics due to their ability to understand and generate human-like text. These models utilize advanced NLP techniques and ML algorithms to analyze, predict, and generate human language text [14]. These models are called "large" because they are built with a vast amount of parameters—often in the billions—which allow them to process and generate coherent and contextually relevant text [15]. LLMs use neural network architectures, particularly the Transformer model, to handle a variety of natural language processing tasks. By understanding the nuances of human language and context, LLMs can be used to extract valuable insights from unstructured data sources, such as customer feedback, product reviews, and social media interactions [14–16].

Using NLP, organizations can analyze historical customer reviews to understand the sentiments and opinions expressed about products. Cognitive analytics can help understand the nuances and sentiment expressed in the text instead of simple keyword matching. Similarly, through NLP and cognitive analytics, customer interaction and feedback can be analyzed in real time from diverse data sources, such as interactions with chatbots or customer service representatives. In essence, cognitive analytics can help understand the context of customer queries, identify common issues, and even suggest personalized solutions based on historical data [17]. However, LLMs can provide several benefits over cognitive computing, such as [15, 16, 18]:

- *Advanced language understanding*: LLMs have a better grasp of the nuances of human language due to their extensive size and complexity, leading to more accurate understanding and generation of text. These models can effectively capture linguistic subtleties and context, enabling them to produce more coherent and contextually relevant responses. LLMs can process information while considering broader context, leading to contextually sensitive responses compared to cognitive computing.
- *Versatility*: LLMs can perform various language-related tasks without needing task-specific programming, including translation, summarization, and question-answering. LLMs can effectively analyze and derive meaningful information from diverse data formats, contributing to more comprehensive and accurate data insights compared to conventional approaches.
- *Adaptability*: LLMs can deliver real-time responses and adapt to evolving language patterns and contexts, allowing them to be fine-tuned for specific applications based on user input and access to large datasets. This adaptability allows them to generate timely and relevant insights from dynamic and rapidly changing

---

[2] https://www.techtarget.com/whatis/definition/ChatGPT.

[3] https://www.techtarget.com/searchenterpriseai/definition/BERT-language-model.

[4] https://www.techtarget.com/searchenterpriseai/feature/Claude-AI-vs-ChatGPT-How-do-they-compare.

[5] https://jenni.ai/.

data sources, providing businesses with up-to-date information for informed decision-making.

- *Scalability*: LLMs' performance tends to improve as they are scaled up (in input parameters and training data), leading to emergent abilities not seen in smaller models. Scalability also helps improve their adaptability and responsiveness as these models fine-tune themselves by generating contextually relevant text in real time.

In a nutshell, the fusion of cognitive analytics (LLMs) and ML expedites the process of sifting through data, allowing businesses to discern pertinent information swiftly. For modern complex and dynamic SCs, cognitive analytics can be a pivotal tool for achieving success, offering distinctive insights through the meticulous analysis of extensive datasets. It can facilitate a competitive edge by providing nuanced perspectives into customer preferences and behavior, enabling the creation of personalized experiences that foster customer loyalty by leveraging both structured and unstructured datasets. Additionally, cognitive analytics aids in identifying new customers by predicting future needs based on market trends and customer data from external sources such as social media feeds. It enhances customer service efficiency by automating routine tasks, contributing to quick query resolution, and increasing customer satisfaction. Moreover, its application in risk management, especially in industries like finance, allows for swift identification and mitigation of potential risks by processing diverse data types [17, 19]. Ultimately, cognitive analytics significantly enhances overall business productivity and efficiency by leveraging predictive insights for strategic decision-making and resource optimization.

3.2.5 A Synergy of Descriptive, Predictive, Prescriptive, and Cognitive Analytics

A comprehensive fusion of descriptive, predictive, prescriptive, and cognitive analytics empowered by LLMs can equip SC operations to gain profound insights into historical trends, forecast future demands, and optimize processes. The outcome is an adaptable and responsive SC harmonizing with evolving customer expectations. This enhances overall customer satisfaction and streamlines operational efficiency, positioning the organization at the forefront of competitiveness within the ever-changing SC landscape.

Let us explore the interconnected narrative of descriptive, predictive, prescriptive, and cognitive analytics through a hypothetical scenario involving a major online retailer. The initial analytical phases start with data exploration by delving into historical data; the retailer can analyze transactional data to understand the time series behavior (trend, seasonality, special events, etc.) and product popularity. The retailer can further analyze customer demographic information, purchase frequencies, spend analysis, average basket size, etc. This becomes the fuel for informed decision-making. It is not merely about deciphering what was bought but understanding why, how, and by whom. This strategic deployment of descriptive analytics unravels historical sales dynamics and lays the groundwork for predictive and prescriptive analytics to refine further and optimize the SC journey.

Organizations can utilize LLMs, advanced AI/ML algorithms, and statistical analysis to forecast the impending demand for products and adjust orders and inventory levels to account for factors like seasonality, trends, holidays, special events, etc. With predictive insights in hand, the journey progresses to prescriptive analytics, where the organization moves beyond anticipating demand to optimize its SC operations proactively. For instance, as the holiday season approaches, the retailer employs prescriptive analytics to optimize its SC operations, such as warehouse space and transportation capacity, to meet the predicted demand while minimizing costs. This includes recommendations on where to hold inventory, how much stock to maintain for each SKU, and which routes to activate for efficient distribution.

Now, envision the integration of cognitive analytics and LLMs into this retail SC example. A cognitive system equipped with LLMs and AI & ML algorithms continuously learns and adapts to the evolving market dynamics. By comprehending the unstructured data, such as customer reviews and social media sentiments, to gauge the popularity of products and identify emerging trends in real time, particularly LLMs can adapt and scale in real time by incorporating the real-time information from customers. The system proactively suggests adjustments to the marketing strategy or introduces new products based on this dynamic understanding.

3.3   Importance of Analytics Models in Driving Customer-Centricity

3.3.1   Leveraging Descriptive Analytics for Customer-Centricity

The customer-centric strategy revolves around building strong customer relationships by consistently delivering exceptional experiences. It necessitates a fundamental shift from product-centric approaches to customer-focused ones. Collecting and analyzing customer data such as buying behavior and interests has become vital in understanding customer needs and fostering meaningful connections at the right moments. In the era of big data (BD), digital technologies, such as advanced Point-of-Sale (POS) systems, Internet of Things (IoT), user-generated content from search and social media, and cloud computing, have led to an unprecedented surge in the volume and diversity of consumer data that companies can collect [20]. In the past, customer demand was primarily understood through sales data. However, with the prevalence of connected devices, such as smartphones and wearables, extensive data is generated even before customers purchase. Figure 3.2 depicts a simplified

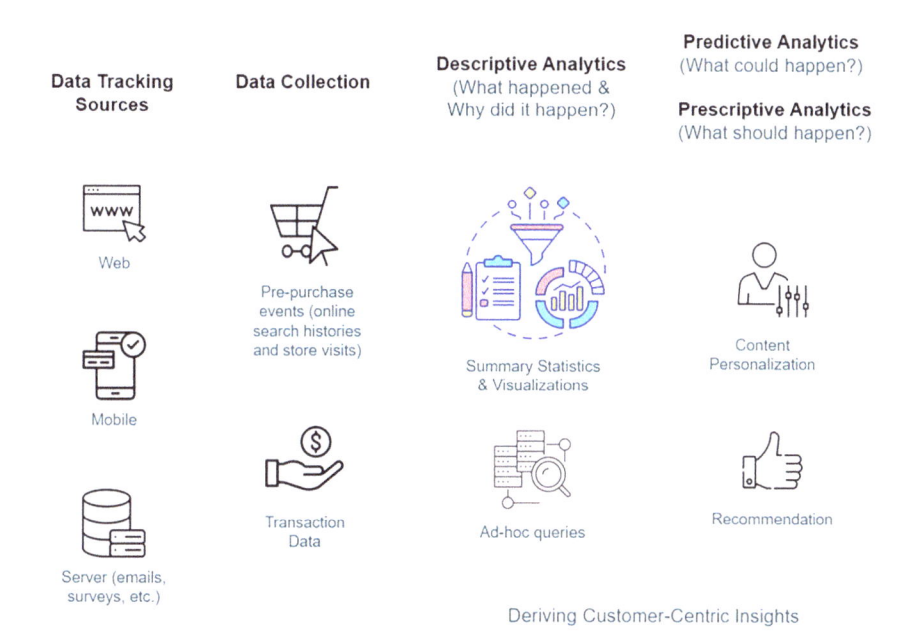

Fig. 3.2 Data analytics solution architecture

data analytics solution architecture, encompassing all possible data tracking sources, such as websites, mobile applications, emails, and surveys. In the Data Collection stage, all consumer behavior events, including online search histories (e.g., page browsing durations, time, and location), store visits, sales, and product returns, are essential data to be collected and analyzed.

In pursuing customer-centric insights, descriptive analytics is the foundational layer when applying analytics models. For instance, retailers use proximity-based technologies like beacons to track in-store customer movements, facilitating accurate personalization and sales optimization [21, 22]. In the online setting, retailers like Amazon have long been analyzing transaction data to detect co-purchase patterns, recommending frequently bought-together products as relevant suggestions. However, this traditional association rule applies only to complementary products. It may not identify substitute product patterns, like recommending Samsung TVs as alternatives to LG TVs, because customers do not typically purchase substitutes together. In order to offer useful substitute product information, recommendation engines must collect and analyze customers' historical web browsing data, requiring additional efforts for descriptive analyses [3].

Despite the wealth of data, effectively extracting valuable insights from the complex data pool remains a formidable challenge. By leveraging the power of descriptive analytics and complementing it with advanced analytical models, companies can truly embrace a customer-centric approach and gain a competitive edge in today's data-driven market.

3.3.2 Harnessing Predictive Analytics for Customer-Centric Supply Chains

As we delve into the realm of predictive analytics for cultivating customer-centric SCs, the focus shifts from understanding past customer behavior (descriptive analytics) to anticipating future needs and preferences. Predictive analytics becomes a strategic tool, enabling organizations to respond to customer expectations proactively and shape SC strategies that are not just reactive but anticipatory and aligned with evolving consumer demands [23, 24]. Predictive analytics for customer-centric SCs involves using data analysis techniques and advanced algorithms to anticipate future trends, behaviors, and demands of customers. It combines historical and real-time data to make informed predictions that guide SC strategies to enhance customer experiences and satisfaction. From a customer-centric perspective, predictive analytics goes beyond time series analysis or statistical forecasting methods. Consider a retail scenario where predictive analytics is employed to optimize the SC for enhanced customer-centricity. By leveraging customer lifetime value modeling, the organization can identify high-value customers and tailor personalized offers to nurture long-term relationships. Churn prediction enables proactive retention strategies, ensuring potential churners engage with targeted initiatives before disengagement occurs [25]. Supervised and unsupervised ML methods can be applied for customer lifetime value analysis. For instance [26, 27],

- Supervised ML approaches (such as Random Forest and Decision Tree regressors) and statistical models (such as Linear, Ridge, or Lasso regression) can be used to predict the monetary value a customer will generate over the lifetime. Similarly, time series models such as ARIMA (Auto-Regressive Integrated Moving Average) and Exponential Smoothing methodscan be used to predict customer spending over time. Organizations can use predictive analytics to anticipate fluctuations in customer demand, allowing for agile adjustments to inventory levels to improve service levels.
- Supervised and unsupervised ML approaches can also be used for customer segmentation through classification models, which is crucial for achieving customer-centricity in various ways. By segmenting customers into distinct groups based on behavior, preferences, and characters, businesses can tailor their strategies to meet the unique needs of each segment. This can help improve overall customer experience through tailored product recommendations, targeted marketing campaigns, personalized customer experiences, optimized customer services, product development and innovation, etc. Some of the ML approaches applicable to customer segmentation include K-Nearest Neighbors (KNN), Decision Trees/ Random Forest, Bayesian Classifiers, K-means clustering, etc.
- From a customer-centricity perspective, association rule mining can be used to discover meaningful associations between different products and services that customers tend to purchase together. Association rule mining is a data mining technique that aims to discover interesting relationships, patterns, or associations

among a set of variables in a large dataset. Through association rule mining, businesses can make informed decisions about product recommendations through

- *Cross-selling*: Recommending complementary products to customers during checkout can increase the likelihood of additional purchases and enhance the overall shopping experience.
- *Bundling*: Analysis of historical purchases can help identify the product or service categories that can be sold together. For example, customers who purchase a laptop often buy laptop accessories as well. The company can create bundled offerings that align with the identified patterns, providing customers with convenient and personalized product bundles. This enhances the customer's shopping experience by anticipating their needs and preferences.
- *Inventory management*: This information can also be leveraged to enhance in-store customer purchasing experience. Items that are purchased together on a frequent basis can be placed close to each other. For example, customers who purchase milk often buy bread as well. This not only improves the shopping experience but also increases inventory management efficiency.

3.3.3 Enabling Prescriptive Analytics in Customer-Centric Supply Chains

Prescriptive analytics is a more advanced form of analytics that suggests the best settings or courses of action to optimize SC performance. It can benefit strategic and operational levels by employing aggregate and granular (day-to-day) data. A pragmatic approach for organizations with evolving analytics capabilities involves initially embracing descriptive and predictive analytics. As data and competency grow, companies progressively advance toward higher-level analytics capabilities, eventually incorporating prescriptive analytics into their strategic decision-making process. This phased adoption ensures a solid foundation, allowing businesses to harness the benefits of analytics while mitigating potential challenges associated with prescriptive analytics [28, 29]. Descriptive and predictive analytics can also directly assist prescriptive analytics by enabling a robust estimate and setup of model variables and parameters. Real-time BD gathering through IoT devices can ensure the relevance of the information used to set up and run the models and improve the accuracy of predictions [30].

Prescriptive analytics coupled with BD have a wide range of utilities, including optimizing sourcing, production, inventory, distribution and transportation, selling, and after-sales servicing. By acquiring demand and supply visibility between downstream and upstream, a manufacturer can optimize its SC decisions, ranging from customer fulfillment to input sourcing and replenishments. For optimum sourcing, data related to supplier risk, delivery performance, and product characteristics can be used to select the best sourcing channels. Analytics can be used to decide the most efficient mix of joint replenishment or single sourcing. For production management, workforce analytics can be employed to optimize labor scheduling to reduce costs while maintaining desired service levels [31].

Radio Frequency Identification (RFID) can enable automatic counting, continuous review, and shrinkage tracking on the inventory management front. Besides eliminating the cost of manual counting, the switch from periodic to continuous review policies can achieve superior performance against inventory holding, ordering, and back-ordering costs [32]. RFID technology can also track inventory in motion, capturing location and quantity. This can have important implications in cold chains where ambient temperature and transit duration can be tracked and used in models to plan optimal order quantities against a service level and create alteration as soon as a problem is detected [31]. On shop floors, RFIDs can be used to convert production resources into smart manufacturing objects capable of interacting with each other to create a ubiquitous environment. Such an environment can generate a large amount of data to support production scheduling and planning optimization. However, estimating delivery times on shop floors is critical for production planning and scheduling to be effective. Production efficiency heavily relies on the arrival of materials. Hence, knowing logistics trajectories is vital [33]. For this, GPS-enabled BD telematics can be used for tracking and route and transportation optimization. The data can enable the optimization of fuel efficiency, preventive maintenance, driver behavior, and vehicle routing. Data for tracking disruptive events, such as weather and traffic incidents, can be used for re-optimization of logistics and transport in real time. For example, UPS uses such data to enable its On-Road Integrated Optimization and Navigation (ORION) system to assist drivers in finding the most efficient route in their delivery areas [31].

At the downstream, i.e., sales and maintenance, the high granularity of data on pricing and sales can enable price optimization. Pricing decisions can be optimized in real time, considering real-time demand patterns, stock availability, weather, and events that can influence a product's demand [31]. Data from tracking and monitoring tools can be used to assist location allocation optimization and on-shelf stock availability [30]. Finally, BD can be used for product design by monitoring up-to-date customer behavior and informing the customers' expectations and opinions. Once data is collected and analyzed, engineering design transforms customer needs into design specifications [4]. With an in-depth understanding of product specifications and data gathering on product use at customer sites, enhanced product reliability can be offered to clients by optimizing asset inspection, maintenance, and repair [31].

3.3.4   Unleashing Cognitive Analytics for Customer-Centricity

Businesses increasingly turn to cognitive analytics to unravel the complex challenge of devising algorithms or establishing rules to comprehend vast datasets. Once companies amass substantial data, a specialized approach becomes imperative to distill essential insights. Some of these examples include:

- *Sentiment analysis*: Organizations (such as Amazon) significantly emphasize understanding customer satisfaction levels and needs. By leveraging sentiment analysis, Amazon gains valuable insights into customer sentiment, preferences, and expectations, allowing the company to deliver personalized experiences, optimize its products and services, and maintain a customer-centric approach. Analyzing social media posts, customer feedback, recommendations, or online reviews to determine the overall sentiments (positive, negative, or neutral) related to a product, service, or brand (Fig. 3.3) can help improve customer service and design products and services based on the "voice of the customer" (VoC) [35].
- *Topic modeling*: Organizations use NLP algorithms to identify and extract themes from a collection of unstructured text documents, enabling them to understand the main subjects discussed. This can play an important role in understanding customer needs and issues by analyzing customer feedback, reviews, and commonly discussed topics with customer chats or transcripts to enhance products, services, and customer experience. Further, customers can be segmented into similar topics to customize products and services and provide personalized recommendations. Topic modeling can also help create a customer journey by analyzing the customer interactions across various touch points such as chat, email, phone, website, etc., and organizations can enhance customer experience and create seamless interaction by optimizing the touchpoints.
- *Image and video tagging*: This refers to applying image recognition algorithms to unstructured image and video data to identify and tag objects, scenes, or

Fig. 3.3 Sample sentiment analysis—brand monitoring [34]

people, making them easily searchable and categorizable. Tagging can enable real-time inventory tracking by identifying products, SKUs, and associated attributes from the visual data to improve stock availability and customer fulfillment. Retailers, such as Tescos,[6] can analyze the empty bins using data collected from video feeds to trigger the restocking processes at the store level, leading to increased customer satisfaction and service levels [36]. Amazon Go is another prime example of companies revolutionizing customer-centric SCs. In Amazon Go[7] stores, customers can enter, shop for products, and simply walk out without going through a traditional checkout process. Through cameras, sensors, and edge devices, items are tracked and added to the customer's virtual cart. The customer is automatically charged based on the items in the virtual cart when a customer leaves the store. This eliminates manual scanning by recognizing the products through image analysis. At the same time, the system can trigger restocking by analyzing products taken from the shelves, enhancing the customer shopping experience. Overall, image and video tagging can help [36, 37]:

- Improve quality assurance by identifying defects and irregularities.
- Personalize products and services based on customer interactions and individual customers.
- Provide a safer and more secure environment by tracking fraudulent activities.

- *Speech-to-text transcription*: This refers to converting unstructured audio data, such as recorded interviews or customer service calls, into structured text transcripts for analysis and insights; some examples include Microsoft Teams, Google Meets, and Siri, all of which allow real-time speech-to-text conversion. Similarly, speech-to-text transcription can be used to analyze customer feedback from recorded calls or surveys to understand themes, sentiments, and complaints. From a customer-centric perspective, customer service calls can be analyzed to identify improvement and training opportunities for service agents. Sentiment analysis can help identify customer emotions during the call and provide valuable insights about the product/service and processes.

---

[6]Tesco plc is a British multinational groceries and general merchandise retailer headquartered in Welwyn Garden City, England. https://www.tescoplc.com/about/.

[7]https://www.amazon.com/b?ie=UTF8&node=16008589011.

3.4 Leveraging Blockchain Technology for Increased Transparency and Trust in Supply Chains

3.4.1 Blockchain

Blockchain is an open distributed ledger that can record transactions between parties efficiently and in a verifiable and permanent way [38]. Blockchain technology (BCT) provides a set of parameters and protocols, that are different from the legacy system, and technology in sharing information, making decisions, and securing records without relying on a central third party.

In essence, blockchain can be characterized as a collection of chronological records of transactions linked with each other (traceability), shared among all parties in the peer-to-peer network (distributed), and verified by a group of participants in the network (decentralized) using a consensus mechanism (consensus). Once the verification is made, the blockchain remains strongly resistant to alteration (immutability) and is protected using cryptography (security), maintaining a single source of truth.

A step-by-step process of a typical business transaction's entry, validation, and recording onto blockchain follows the general sequence depicted in Fig. 3.4. While this digital record-keeping technology has found plenty of use cases in the financial sector, businesses also agree that it holds the highest potential value in SCM [39]. With its ability to facilitate the use of smart contracts in SC transactions, BCT has

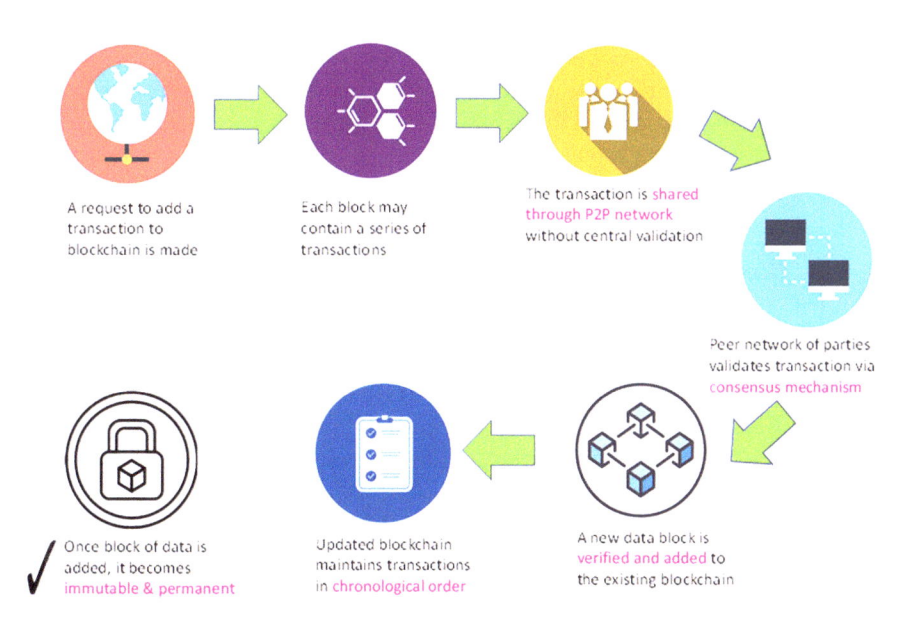

Fig. 3.4 A step-by-step process of a transaction using blockchain technology

proved it holds significant value with regard to transparency, traceability, and accountability across the whole SC, from the source to the end customers.

3.4.2 Smart Contracts

Smart contracts are digital agreements that self-execute once a consensus on a conditioned event (or transaction) is validated and recorded on blockchain [40]. With blockchain's shared IT infrastructure and increased transparency in place, smart contracts not only facilitate business partners to agree on details of transactions but also streamline workflows for all parties involved within the SC, minimizing duplication efforts. For instance, a major consortium blockchain comprising AB InBev, Accenture, APL, Kuhne Nagel, and a European customs organization tested a blockchain solution developed by Accenture to assess the improvement in document processing for international shipments of automotive, retail, and consumer goods [41]. International shipment is a document-heavy process, typically requiring over 20 paper-based documents to move goods from exporter to importer. Across these documents, up to 70% of data involves duplication or replication according to the test run, undermining data quality and real-time visibility. Overall, the blockchain solution implemented showed that it could reduce data entry requirements by up to 80% and simplify data amendments across the process, significantly reducing errors while speeding up the process.

Further, blockchain's improved transparency and decentralized validation process have led to the elevation of trust among SC partners in the consortium. Blockchain is known as a trustless system, implying that one can have confidence in the validity of transactions without trusting the integrity of any individuals, intermediaries, or governments, as the trust is now transferred from one central authority to many decentralized parties in the network [42] which, in turn, can potentially lead to the prevention of single point of failure.

3.4.3 Blockchain Technology Use Cases in the Supply Chain

Below are some of the successful implementations of BCT in different SC sectors:

- *Food SC*: Built on the IBM blockchain, IBM Food Trust connects SC partners (manufacturers, wholesalers, retailers, growers, processors, etc.) by sharing a trusted record of food provenance, further enhancing visibility, accuracy, and accountability of transaction data in the food SC. Companies using IBM Food Trust include Walmart, Nestle, Golden State Foods, and Dole Food Company [43].
- *Fashion SC*: Fashion designer Martine Jarlgaard collaborated with blockchain service Provenance to monitor the supply of garments. Suppliers could connect and transfer assets with end-to-end visibility in their SC using the Provenance

blockchain app. BCT could also be used to address growing concerns about the working conditions of the garment manufacturing industry globally [44].

- *Fishing industry*: TraSeable Solutions, a Fijian blockchain service working in partnership with the World Wildlife Fund (WWF) and Consensys, provided sustainable solutions to tuna fishing in the Western and Central Pacific [45]. This partnership created one of the first blockchain ventures to detect the problems of illegal fishing. TraSeable enabled customers to gather data on harvests, catch logs, crew details, and fishing ground analytics using a smartphone app to help minimize illegal or unethical fishing practices.
- *Pharmaceutical SC*: Existing approaches implemented to ensure traceability in the pharmaceutical SC are often centralized, lacking transparency throughout the transit process. This has undermined public confidence in pharmaceutical SC processes, especially with the increased cases of counterfeit medication. Using smart contracts, blockchain-based platforms, such as PharmaChain, can eliminate data fragmentation between different entities by creating a trail of a secure, single source of truth for the entire life cycle of medicine [46]. Another blockchain service, Modum, based in Switzerland, designed a safe transit process for drugs sensitive to environmental changes. It used smart contracts to assess the compliance requirement (regarding the temperature) of the products to be delivered [47].

Other blockchain use cases in SC sectors can be found in the diamond SC (e.g., to monitor mining conditions or quality), the fruit and vegetable SC (e.g., to monitor organic status via the use of smart contracts), the wine SC (e.g., to detect counterfeit wine), and the energy SC (e.g., to improve transparency) among others.

3.4.4 Blockchain-Driven Big Data Analytics

The practical use of blockchain-driven smart contracts based on the immutability feature of BCT is plentiful in various supply chain sectors, as discussed above. However, BCT application in big data analytics (BDA) is still in a nascent stage [48, 49] with limited use cases in the financial, health, and supply chain sectors [50, 51]. Now, with the new level of opportunities opened up with the application of BCT in data management and data-driven decisions, potential added value in BDA is expected to escalate significantly in use cases across descriptive, predictive, prescriptive, and cognitive analytics [49, 52]:

- *Descriptive analytics*: In descriptive analytics, where historical data is crucial, blockchain's immutability ensures that it cannot be altered once data is recorded. This feature enhances the reliability of historical records and supports the visualization of accurate snap shots, trends, and data patterns.
- *Predictive analytics*: In predictive analytics, accurate and trustworthy data is paramount for forecasting. Blockchain ensures that data used in predictive models is sourced from trusted and verifiable origins. Based on this, businesses

leverage predictive analytics to make informed decisions and create fact-based contingency plans with improved reliability and accuracy [53].

- *Prescriptive analytics*: In prescriptive analytics, where recommendations are made for optimal actions, smart contracts can be programmed to execute recommended strategies automatically across different supply chain tiers. With the importance of cross-functional strategies and impacts highlighted for prescriptive analytics, the trust relations based on the decentralized structure of blockchain add speed and efficiency to decision-making processes while reducing potential vulnerabilities in contract execution [54].
- *Cognitive analytics*: Cognitive analytics relies on diverse and often unstructured data. Blockchain's decentralized and distributed ledger allows different parties to collaborate on data analysis without compromising data security. This collaborative and secure environment can enhance the quality of insights derived from cognitive analytics. In addition, using a secure and immutable ledger containing past customer service interactions, cognitive analytics can provide personalized and detailed customer service solutions tailored to each customer's preferences [55].

Further, there are other synergistic benefits manifested in BDA powered by BCT implementation:

- *Cross-organizational data sharing*: In a series of supply chain transactions that entail numerous stakeholders, the distributed nature of BCT enables data sharing across different organizations within a consortium blockchain, where the chronological records of transactions remain fully intact as every node (or entity) maintains the same copy of the ledger providing a single source of truth. This allows multiple entities in the supply chain to gain access to the stored dataset in the blockchain and develop insights in making decisions in CCSSC, with full confidence in the integrity of the dataset [39].
- *Data privacy and security*: In analytics, sensitive information is often involved. The enhanced security measures provided by blockchain technology protect against unauthorized access and data breaches, ensuring the privacy and confidentiality of data. Data security in BCT refers to the ability of a blockchain network to defend itself against any coordinated and malicious attacks, such as distributed denial-of-service (DDoS attacks). It is one of the most significant benefits BCT has to offer to BDA [56].

In summary, BCT provides a foundation for trust, security, and collaboration in the realm of BDA. Its decentralized and transparent nature addresses key data management and integrity challenges, ultimately enhancing the value and reliability of descriptive, predictive, perspective, and cognitive analytics across various industries.

References

1. IBM. (n.d.). What is supply chain management? Retrieved August 8, 2023, from https://www.ibm.com/topics/supply-chain-management

2. Inferenz. (2023, June 7). AI and predictive analytics in supply chain management: Revolutionizing efficiency and optimization. LinkedIn. Retrieved August 8, 2023, from https://www.linkedin.com/pulse/ai-predictive-analytics-supply-chain-management-revolutionizing/

3. Duan, L., & Xu, L. D. (2021). Data analytics in industry 4.0: A survey. *Information Systems Frontiers, 1*, 1–17. https://doi.org/10.1007/s10796-021-10190-0

4. Retail bi-platform with AI and Computer Vision. Retail BI Platform with AI and Computer Vision. (n.d.). Retrieved July 31, 2023, from https://www.itransition.com/portfolio/bi-platform-for-a-large-fashion-retailer

5. Chong, D., & Shi, H. (2015). Big data analytics: A literature review. *Journal of Management Analytics, 2*(3), 175–201. https://doi.org/10.1080/23270012.2015.1082449

6. Khatri, V., & Samuel, B. M. (2019). Analytics for managerial work. *Communications of the ACM, 62*(4), 100. https://doi.org/10.1145/3274277

7. Silva, A. J., Cortez, P., Pereira, C., & Pilastri, A. (2021). Business analytics in industry 4.0: A systematic review. *Expert Systems, 38*(7), e12741. https://doi.org/10.1111/exsy.12741

8. Santosh, S. (2022). End-to-end predictive analysis on Uber's data. Analytics Vidhya. Retrieved Sept 12, 2023, from https://www.analyticsvidhya.com/blog/2021/10/end-to-end-predictive-analysis-on-ubers-data/

9. ProjectPro. (n.d.). How big data analysis helped increase Walmart's sales turnover? Retrieved September 3, 2023, from https://www.projectpro.io/article/how-big-data-analysis-helped-increase-walmarts-sales-turnover/109

10. Pandey, V. (2023). Unlocking the power of AI and ML: How retailers are transforming the shopping experience. LinkedIn. Retrieved September 3, 2023, from https://www.linkedin.com/pulse/unlocking-power-ai-ml-how-retailers-transforming-shopping-pandey-1f

11. Davenport, D. H. (2006). Competing on Analytics. Analytics and data science - Harvard Business Review. Retrieved Aug 15, 2023, from https://hbr.org/2006/01/competing-on-analytics

12. Gudivada, V. N., Irfan, M. T., Fathi, E., & Rao, D. L. (2016). Cognitive analytics: Going beyond big data analytics and machine learning. *Handbook of Statistics, 35*, 169–205. https://doi.org/10.1016/bs.host.2016.07.010

13. Trexin Insight Paper. (2022). Cognitive analytics - The next wave of analytics in data science (pp. 1–4), Retrieved Sept 12, 2023, from COGNITIVE ANALYTICS | Trexin Consulting.

14. Bzdok, D., Thieme, A., Levkovskyy, O., Wren, P., Ray, T. S., & Reddy, S. (2024). Data science opportunities of large language models for neuroscience and biomedicine. *Neuron, 112*(5), 698–717. https://doi.org/10.1016/j.neuron.2024.01.016

15. Huang, J., Gu, S., Hou, L., Wu, Y., Wang, X., Yu, H., & Han, J. (2022). *Large language models can self-improve*. Cornell University. https://doi.org/10.48550/arxiv.2210.11610

16. Shanahan, M. (2024). Talking about large language models. *Association for Computing Machinery, 67*(2), 68–79. https://doi.org/10.1145/3624724

17. Sharma, S. (2023). *Leveraging cognitive analytics for competitive advantage*. Markovate Information Blog. Retrieved Dec 5, 2023, from https://markovate.com/blog/cognitive-analytics/

18. Lee, A. (2023, January 26). What are large language models used for and why are they important? Retrieved April 7, 2024, from https://blogs.nvidia.com/blog/what-are-large-language-models-used-for/

19. Insight Desk. (2023). Cognitive analytics: Transforming data into actionable insights. Deman Talk. Retrieved December 5, 2023, from https://www.demandtalk.com/insights/data/analytics/cognitive-analytics-transforming-data-into-actionable-insights/

20. Boone, T., Ganeshan, R., Jain, A., & Sanders, N. R. (2019). Forecasting sales in the supply chain: Consumer analytics in the big data era. *International Journal of Forecasting, 35*(1), 170–180. https://doi.org/10.1016/j.ijforecast.2018.09.003

21. Cohen, M. C. (2018). Big data and service operations. *Production and Operations Management, 27*(9), 1709–1723. https://doi.org/10.1111/poms.12832

22. Feng, Q., & Shanthikumar, J. G. (2018). How research in production and operations management may evolve in the era of big data. *Production and Operations Management, 27*(9), 1670–1784. https://doi.org/10.1111/poms.12836

23. Punia, S., & Shankar, S. (2022). Predictive analytics for demand forecasting: A deep learning-based decision support system. *Knowledge-Based Systems, 258*(11), 1–15. https://doi.org/10.1016/j.knosys.2022.109956

24. Chen, Y., Li, C., & Wang, H. (2022). Big data and predictive analytics for business intelligence: A bibliographic study (2000–2021). *Forecast, 4*(4), 767–786. https://doi.org/10.3390/forecast4040042

25. Aslekar, A., Sahu, P., & Pahari, A. (2019). Big data analytics for customer lifetime value prediction. *Telecom Business Review, 12*(1), 46–49.

26. Shmueli, G., Bruce, P. C., Gedeck, P., & Patel, N. R. (2020). *Data mining for business analytics: Concepts, techniques and applications in Python*. John Wiley & Sons.

27. Tipi, N. (2020). *Supply chain analytics and modelling: Quantitative tools and applications*. Kogan Page.

28. Arunachalam, D., Kumar, N., & Kawalek, J. P. (2017). Understanding big data analytics capabilities in supply chain management: Unravelling the issues, challenges and implications for practice. *Transportation Research Part E: Logistics and Transportation Review., 114*, 416–436. https://doi.org/10.1016/j.tre.2017.04.001

29. Nguyen, T., Zhou, L., Spiegler, V., Ieromonachou, P., & Lin, Y. (2018). Big data analytics in supply chain management: A state-of-the-art literature review. *Computers & Operations Research, 98*, 254–264. https://doi.org/10.1016/j.cor.2017.07.004

30. Talwar, S., Kaur, P., Fosso Wamba, S., & Dhir, A. (2021). Big data in operations and supply chain management: A systematic literature review and future research agenda. *International Journal of Production Research, 59*(11), 3509–3534. https://doi.org/10.1080/00207543.2020.1868599

31. Sanders, N. R. (2016). How to use big data to drive your supply chain. *California Management Review, 58*(3), 26–48. https://doi.org/10.1525/cmr.2016.58.3.26

32. Çakıcı, Ö. E., Groenevelt, H., & Seidmann, A. (2011). Using RFID for the management of pharmaceutical inventory—System optimization and shrinkage control. *Decision Support Systems, 51*(4), 842–852. https://doi.org/10.1016/j.dss.2011.02.003

33. Zhong, R. Y., Huang, G. Q., Lan, S., Dai, Q. Y., Chen, X., & Zhang, T. (2015). A big data approach for logistics trajectory discovery from RFID-enabled production data. *International Journal of Production Economics, 165*, 260–272. https://doi.org/10.1016/j.ijpe.2015.02.014

34. Determ. (2023). Top 5 examples of sentiment analysis. Retrieved Oct 25, 2023, from https://www.determ.com/blog/top-5-examples-of-sentiment-analysis/

35. Rana, D. S. (2021). Amazon review data analysis with sentiment mining. Amazon Review Data Analysis with Sentiment Mining. Retrieved Sept 12, 2023, from https://www.repustate.com/blog/amazon-review-analysis/

36. HBR. (2016). Tesco: A digital transformation. Technology and Operations Management. Retrieved Sept 12, 2023, from https://d3.harvard.edu/platform-rctom/submission/tesco-a-digital-transformation/

37. Tyagi, N. (n.d.). 5 ways Tesco uses big data Analytics. Analytics Steps. Retrieved Sept 12, 2023, from https://www.analyticssteps.com/blogs/5-ways-tesco-uses-big-data-analytics

38. Iansiti, M., & Lakhani, K. R. (2017). The truth about blockchain. *Harvard Business Review, 95*(1), 118–127.

39. Gaur, V., & Gaiha, A. (2020). Building a transparent supply chain. *Harvard Business Review, 98*(2), 94–103.

40. Cong, L., & Klotz, F. (2018). Navigating the next wave of blockchain innovation: Smart contracts. *MIT Sloan Management Review*, 1–7. Available at: https://sloanreview.mit.edu/article/navigating-the-next-wave-of-blockchain-innovation-smart-contracts/

41. Henderson, J. (2020). Industry consortium successfully tests "revolutionary" Accenture blockchain solution. Supply Chain Digital. Retrieved September 10, 2023, from https://supplychaindigital.com/technology/industry-consortium-successfully-tests-revolutionary-accenture-blockchain-solution

42. Werbach, K. (2018). Trust, but verify: Why the blockchain needs the law. *Berkeley Technology Law Journal, 33*(2), 487–550.

43. IBM. (n.d.). IBM food trust. Retrieved October 24, 2023, from https://www.ibm.com/products/supply-chain-intelligence-suite/food-trust

44. Fashion Innovation Agency. (n.d.). Can blockchain revolutionise supply chain transparency within the fashion industry? Retrieved October 24, 2023, from https://www.fialondon.com/projects/martine-jarlgaard-x-provenance-x-a-transparent-company/

45. Rogerson, M., & Parry, G. C. (2020). Blockchain: Case studies in food supply chain visibility. *Supply Chain Management: An International Journal, 25*(5), 601–614. https://doi.org/10.1108/SCM-08-2019-0300

46. Bapatla, A. K., Mohanty, S., Kougianos, E., & Puthal, D. (2023). PharmaChain: Blockchain to ensure counterfeit-free pharmaceutical supply chain. *The Institute of Engineering and Technology, 12*, 53–76. https://doi.org/10.1049/ntw2.12041

47. Gomasta, S. S., Dhali, A., Tahlil, T., Anwar, M. M., & Ali, A. B. M. S. (2023). PharmaChain: Blockchain-based drug supply chain provenance verification system. *Heliyon, 9*(7), 1–15. https://doi.org/10.1016/j.heliyon.2023.e17957

48. Dolgui, A., Ivanov, D., Potryasaev, S., Ivanova, M., & Werner, F. (2020). Blockchain oriented dynamic modelling of smart contract design and execution in the supply chain. *International Journal of Production Research, 58*(7), 2184–2199. https://doi.org/10.1080/00207543.2019.1627439

49. Sundarakani, B., Ajaykumar, A., & Gunasekaran, A. (2021). Big data driven supply chain design and applications for blockchain: An action research using case study approach. *Omega, 102*, 102452. https://doi.org/10.1016/j.omega.2021.102452

50. Muneeza, A., Arshad, N. A., & Arifin, A. T. (2018). The application of blockchain technology in crowdfunding: Towards financial inclusion via technology. *International Journal of Management and Applied Research, 5*(2), 82–98. https://doi.org/10.18646/2056.52.18-007

51. Omar, A. A., Bhuiyan, M. Z. A., Basu, A., Kiyomoto, S., & Rahman, M. S. (2019). Privacy-friendly platform for healthcare data in cloud based on blockchain environment. *Future Generation Computer Systems, 95*, 511–521. https://doi.org/10.1016/j.future.2018.12.044

52. Hassani, H., Huang, X., & Silva, E. (2018). Banking with blockchain-ed big data. *Journal of Management Analytics, 5*(4), 256–275. https://doi.org/10.1080/23270012.2018.1528900

53. Schlegel, A., Birkel, H. S., & Hartmann, E. (2021). Enabling integrated business planning through big data analytics: A case study on sales and operations planning. *International Journal of Physical Distribution and Logistics Management, 51*(6), 607–633. https://doi.org/10.1108/IJPDLM-05-2019-0156

54. Khan, S. N., Loukil, F., Ghedira-Guegan, C., Benkhelifa, E., & Bani-Hani, A. (2021). Blockchain smart contracts: Applications, challenges, and future trends. *Peer-to-Peer Networking and Applications, 14*, 2901–2925. https://doi.org/10.1007/s12083-021-01127-0

55. IBM. (n.d.). Improving customer service: How cognitive technology creates value in the contract center. Retrieved Nov 3, 2023, from https://www.ibm.com/watson/advantage-reports/cognitive-business-lessons/customer-service.html#:~:text=In%20fact%2C%20IBM%20research%20shows,service%20as%20a%20top%20outcome.&text=Unlike%20touch%2Dtone%20and%20IVR,patterns%20and%20learning%20from%20experience

56. Teoh, B. P. C. (2022). Chapter 25. Navigating the blockchain trilemma: A supply chain dilemma. In A. In Ismail, W. M. Dahalan, & A. Öchsner (Eds.), *Advanced maritime technologies and applications* (pp. 291–300).

Chapter 4
Achieving Customer-Centricity Through Data Analytics: Case Study on Women's Clothing E-Commerce Reviews

4.1 Case Introduction

The fashion supply chain (SC) typically involves various stages, such as apparel design, supplier selection, material sourcing, manufacturing, distribution, and sales. Figure 4.1 shows one example of a fashion retailer's SC where the retail firm directly conducts business with its tier 1 suppliers. Suppliers in each tier do business with their immediate adjacent tier. Tier 1 suppliers are companies that work with product manufacture and processing. Companies working with component production and processing tend to fall into tiers 2–4. Further upstream in the SC, tiers 4–6 suppliers are responsible for raw material production. Customers purchase apparel products through online channels downstream of the SC.

From the retailer's perspective, various analyses are undertaken to gain insights into customer preferences and feedback. The goal is to use the information generated to guide the retail firm in improving its products and services by implementing SC strategies, ultimately enhancing the shopping experience for customers.

The women's clothing e-commerce review dataset contains 23,486 customer reviews. Detailed descriptions of customer review information are provided in 11 columns as listed in Table 4.1. Reviews correspond to six departments, i.e., Bottoms, Dresses, Intimates, Jackets, Tops, and Trends. One department can include multiple product classes. For instance, the Tops department contains product classes of Blouses, Knits, Sweaters, and Fine Gauge. The Jackets department offers product classes of Outerwear and Jackets.

© The Author(s), under exclusive license to Springer Nature Switzerland AG 2024
P. S. Kang et al., *Service 4.0*, SpringerBriefs in Service Science, https://doi.org/10.1007/978-3-031-63875-6_4

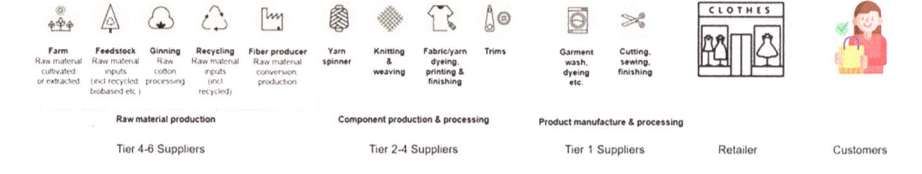

Fig. 4.1 Sample supply chain of a fashion retailer

Table 4.1   Dataset description of the "Women's Clothing E-Commerce Reviews" dataset

Column name	Description	Data type
Transaction ID	Integer variable specifies the transaction number	Whole number
Clothing ID	Integer categorical variable that refers to the specific piece being reviewed	Whole number
Age	Positive integer variable of the reviewer's age, ranging from 18 to 99	Whole number
Title	String variable for the title of the review	Text
Review text	String variable for the review body	Text
Rating	Positive ordinal integer variable for the product score granted by the customer from 1 (worst) to 5 (best)	Whole number
Recommended Ind	Binary variable stating where the customer recommends the product where 1 is recommended, 0 is not recommended	Whole number
Positive feedback count	Positive integer documenting the number of other customers who found this review positive	Whole number
Division name	Categorical name of the product division name	Text
Department name	Categorical name of the product department name	Text
Class name	Categorical name of the product class name	Text

4.2   Case Analyses

We break down our analyses into four typical business inquiries as examples. Answers to these common questions can help the retailer gain a deeper understanding of their customers' preferences, satisfactions, and areas of improvement.

- How are the customers' ratings and recommendations distributed?
- What are the most common words in reviews?
- What are the different words used by customers recommending the clothing compared with those who do not recommend it? Is there any difference in customers' feedback among different departments?
- What are the frequently occurring combinations of words in reviews? What insights can be generated for the retailer to improve the customer experience?

4.2.1 *Distribution of Customer Ratings and Recommendations*

Chapter 3 discusses descriptive analytics as the fundamental method for summarizing "what happened." Figure 4.2 showcases a sample dashboard constructed using Microsoft Power BI, presenting interactive descriptive analytics findings from the women's clothing e-commerce review dataset. The dashboard includes visuals depicting transaction proportions categorized by division, department, and class name. Moreover, it reveals that a higher percentage of customers (82.23%) recommended the clothing products, in contrast to the 17.77% who did not. The majority of customers, approximately 55.91%, provided a top rating of 5, indicating their strong satisfaction. Additionally, a significant portion, 21.62%, was awarded a rating of 4, reflecting a positive sentiment. However, 10.25% of the customers expressed dissatisfaction, assigning a negative rating of 1 or 2.

The sample dashboard is interactive in two ways. First, there is a Q&A visual located at the upper left corner, enabling investigators to ask natural language questions and obtain rapid responses from the dataset. The upper left section in Fig. 4.3 shows an example of the Q&A visual in action, providing results when a question is posed about the class names included in the Tops department.

All the other visuals in the dashboard are interconnected. Applying one or more filters simultaneously affects all the visuals, allowing users to extract a group of insights from a specific subset of the data.

For instance, upon selecting reviews from the Tops department, the dashboard (Fig. 4.3) shows the following results:

- There are 10,468 transactions from the Tops department.

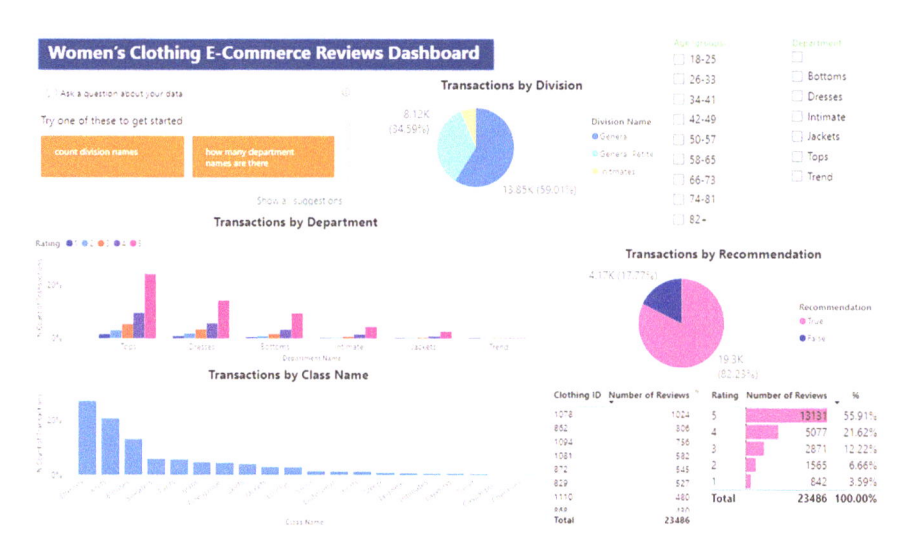

Fig. 4.2 A sample dashboard

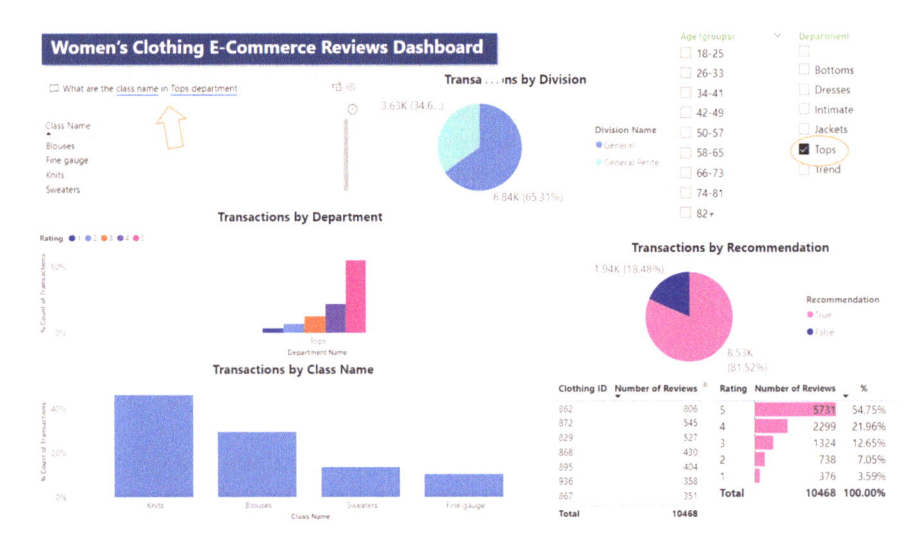

Fig. 4.3 Dashboard results for transactions from Tops department

- Among all Tops department transactions, the majority of the customers (81.52%) recommended clothing products, while 18.48% did not.
- Among all Tops department transactions, more than half of the customers (54.75%) awarded a top rating of 5. The rating distribution is displayed in both the "Transactions by Department" clustered column chart and the table in the lower right section.

By applying two additional filters, specifically targeting reviews with ratings of 1 and 2 in the "Transactions by Department" clustered column chart, the dashboard (Fig. 4.4) reveals the following results:

- A total of 1114 customers expressed dissatisfaction with their purchases from the Tops department.
- Among the 1114 reviews, most customers (1063 customers, or 10.15% of all Tops department purchases) did not recommend the clothing products, whereas only 51 customers (0.49% of all Tops department purchases) recommended the products.
- Among the 1114 reviews, 66.25% of the customers gave a rating of 2, while the remaining 33.75% rated their experience as 1.
- Additionally, the table next to the rating distribution table lists all clothing IDs and their corresponding review counts within the filtered category. For example, Clothing ID 862 received 84 ratings of 1 or 2.

Different filters can be applied to the dashboard to extract summary statistics from various perspectives, such as analyses by age groups. Alternatively, other visuals can be constructed for comparative analyses. Figure 4.5, for example, presents a rating distribution by department.

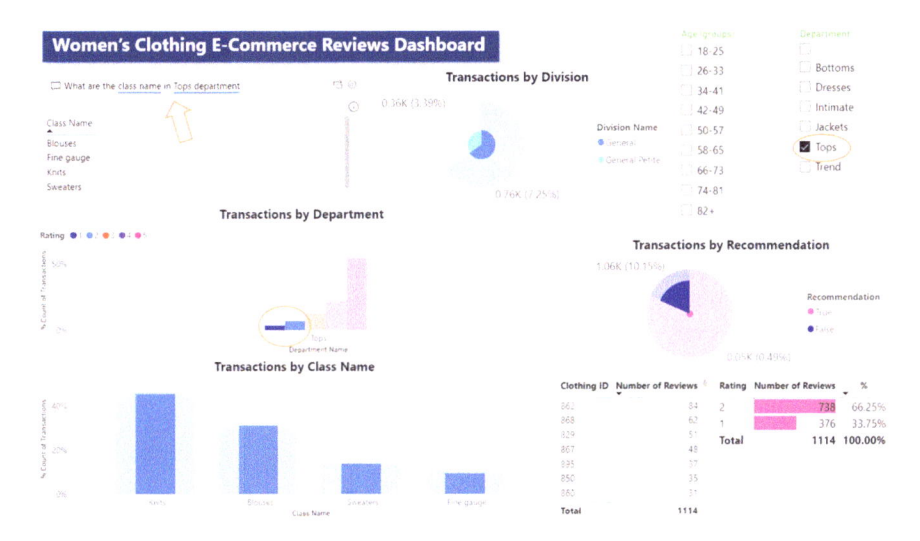

Fig. 4.4 Dashboard results for transactions from Tops department with negative ratings

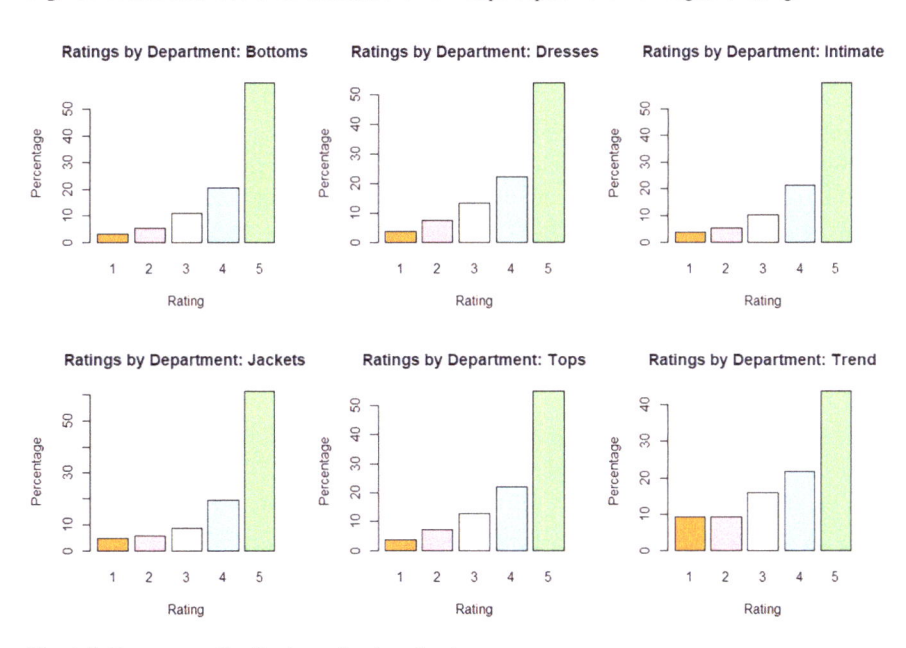

Fig. 4.5 Percentage distributions of ratings by department

Most customer ratings are positive, with a value of 4 or 5. The Trend department seems to receive a greater percentage of negative ratings, 1 or 2. However, by looking into the review counts by department in Table 4.2, it is found that the Trend department only received 119 reviews, which is significantly less than the number of reviews for other departments. The investigator should be aware of this sample

Table 4.2 Number of reviews by department

Department	Bottoms	Dresses	Intimate	Jackets	Tops	Trend
Number of reviews	3799	6319	1735	1032	10,468	119

size difference in making performance comparisons across departments. If more review data could become available, it would be interesting to see whether the proportion of negative ratings for the Trend department decreases to a level similar to that for the other departments or whether the Trend department consistently receives a greater percentage of negative ratings. If the latter is true, more attention should be allocated to analyzing the sources of customer dissatisfaction in the Trend department.

4.2.2   Frequent Words in Reviews

Two columns in the dataset contain customer review information, the title and the review text. Before analyzing the most frequent words, we need to preprocess the text data in the two columns. Preprocessing of textual data usually involves various techniques, including but not limited to:

- Tokenization to create a token for each word.
- Removal of unwanted characters and symbols from the sentences. For example, contractions such as "don't" are expanded to "do not" for better analysis. Texts are all converted into lowercase so machines will interpret the same word consistently.
- Removal of stop words like "a," "an," "the," etc.
- Stemming and lemmatization, which reduces the word to its root stem. For instance, the words "run," "running," "runs," and "ran" are analyzed as a single item, "run."

After preprocessing, we can create word clouds to depict the most frequent words in the review titles and the review texts, respectively. The more frequently a specific word appears in the text, the bigger and bolder it will be in the word cloud.

Figure 4.6 shows the word clouds for all the review titles and review texts, respectively. It provides textual details to reflect that a significant portion of positive customer ratings is mainly associated with comments like "love," "great," "beautiful," and "cute" in the review titles. Words reflecting the look, the size, the color, and the materials frequently appear in the review text, visualizing the most important quality factors women customers care about in selecting clothing.

It is interesting to note that the word with the highest frequency, "dress," however, may not be useful in generating managerial insights. As a result, one additional step must be added in the data preprocessing to exclude words like "dress" and "top" from the analysis. As an alternative visualization tool, Fig. 4.7 depicts a box

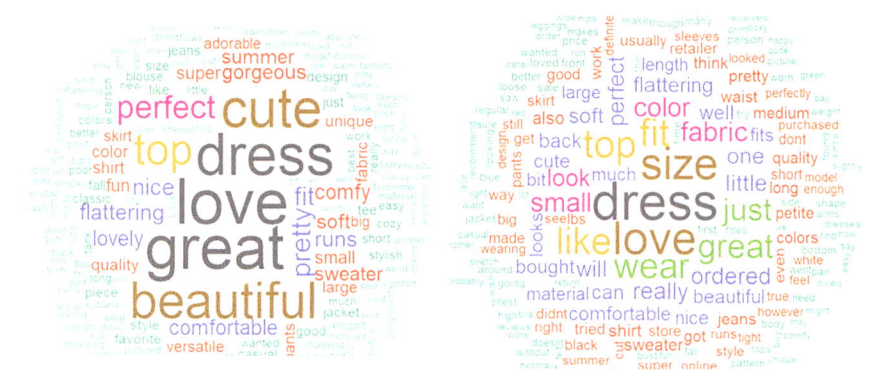

Fig. 4.6 Word clouds for review titles (left) and review text (right)

plot to show the most frequently used words that contain useful information in the review titles.

Based on the words customers used in their reviews, the appearance ("cute," "beautiful," "pretty," etc.), the fit, and the materials ("comfortable," "comfy," and "soft") are critical aspects of clothing that women customers focus on. This particular retailer attracted more positive reviews because it offers better quality in terms of these three aspects.

4.2.3 Comparison of Frequent Words in Reviews

In addition to identifying the most frequent words in all the reviews with a single word cloud, creating a comparison cloud provides investigators with a powerful tool to scrutinize the distinctions and commonalities between two or more subsets of data. Figure 4.8 depicts the frequent words used in the review titles (left) and review texts (right), categorized by the two customer groups giving different recommendations. The results reveal that customers with positive purchase experiences often used words like "love," "great," and "perfect." In contrast, those who did not recommend the clothing products frequently indicated disappointment, product return, and concerns regarding poor quality, fabric, and size.

Figure 4.9 presents another comparison cloud, offering insights into the prevalent words used in review texts, categorized by the six departments. This visualization highlights that customers exhibit distinct priorities and concerns regarding various types of clothing products. For instance, reviews within the Intimate department frequently emphasized the comfort and softness of the materials. In contrast, feedback related to the Tops department primarily centered around clothing color and appearance, while customers from the Bottoms department paid particular attention to aspects such as size, fit, and the stretchiness of the clothing.

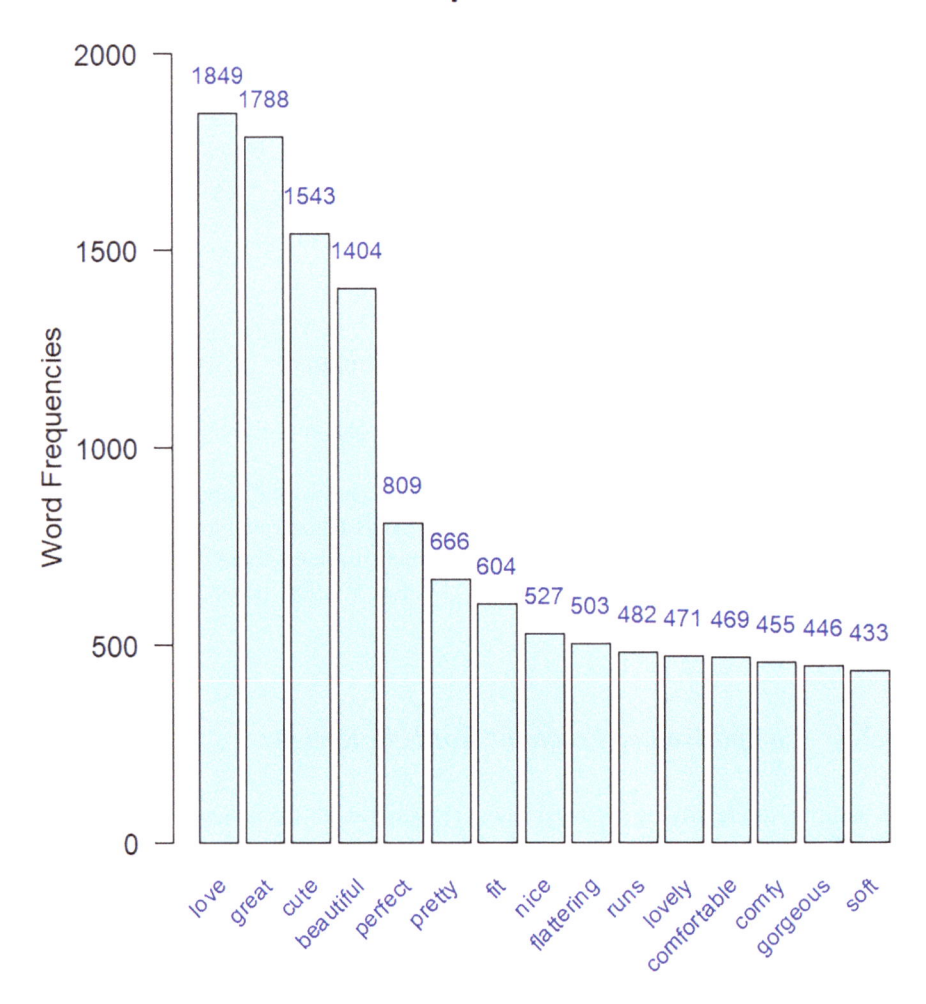

Fig. 4.7 Most frequent words in review titles after removing "dress" and "top"

4.2.4 Frequent Combinations of Words in Reviews

Instead of highlighting one word only, finding important combinations of words in the text data can provide more context and better capture the nuances of language by considering the relationships between adjacent words. Ngram analysis, including bigrams and trigrams, is a fundamental concept in natural language processing (NLP) that plays a crucial role in understanding and analyzing text data. A bigram is a sequence of two consecutive words in a text, while a trigram consists of three adjacent words. Trigrams, in particular, provide more context in analyzing longer-range dependencies and patterns in the text.

Fig. 4.8 Comparison clouds for review titles (left) and review text (right) by customer recommendation

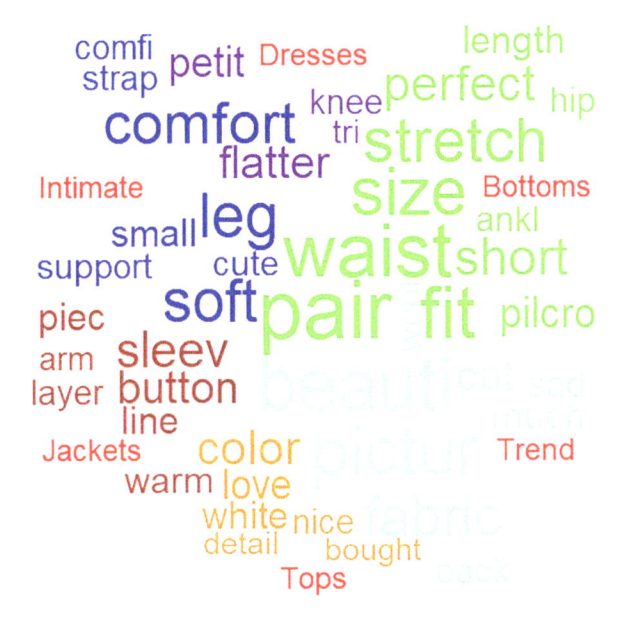

Fig. 4.9 Comparison cloud for review text by department

Using the Tops department review text data with ratings of 1 and 2, a trigram word cloud is generated in Fig. 4.10. It quickly captures several themes within the reviews, including:

Fig. 4.10 Trigram word cloud for tops department review text with negative ratings

- Dissatisfied customers express a desire to return products.
- Incidents of issues either during or immediately after the first use of the clothing.
- Consistent complaints regarding discrepancies between online product displays and the actual appearance of the items.
- Concerns about excessive fabric in the clothing design.

Based on the analyses presented, the fashion retailer can strategically target areas to enhance the customer experience. A significant number of customers who rated Tops products poorly expressed a desire to initiate product returns. It suggests that the retailer needs to thoroughly investigate the underlying reasons for these return requests and seek ways to improve customer satisfaction.

Using the sizing issue as an example, the company can apply *diagnostic analytics* to identify patterns and correlations between specific product characteristics and sizing complaints. For instance, the analysis may reveal that dresses made from a particular stretchy fabric often have more size problems than those made from stiffer materials. Similarly, it may be found that clothes with a specific style are more likely to have complaints about fitting.

By analyzing past transaction data, *predictive analytics* can predict future demand, including quantity and total spending for each clothing category. Furthermore, using historical data on product attributes and corresponding customer complaints, predictive analytics can estimate probabilities of different combinations of factors leading to size problems for each clothing category. For example, it may predict that dresses made from stretchy fabric with a tight cut have a 60%

probability of resulting in size issues. In comparison, dresses made from non-stretchy fabric with a looser fit have only a 20% probability.

Based on the above predictive insights, the e-commerce platform can take proactive measures to mitigate sizing issues. Potential solutions can be divided into non-data-driven and data-driven groups.

- Non-data-driven solutions: The retailer can revise product descriptions to give customers more detailed sizing information or guidance, such as recommending a size up for dresses made from stretchy fabric that fits tightly. Alternatively, the company can invest in augmented reality (AR) applications so customers can virtually try on a dress using their body measurements and see how it might fit. Both strategies help enhance shopping experiences and reduce product return rates.
- Data-driven solutions: Clothing types with higher probabilities of sizing issues may be returned more. To increase customer satisfaction, the retailer can use *prescriptive analytics* to recommend optimal inventory levels, ensuring that items with higher exchange rates are stocked in appropriate quantities. As a more proactive strategy, the company can use simulation to compare possible outcomes of adjusting various factors. To reduce the number of sizing complaints, would the best option be substituting the fabric, improving the size and fit guides, revising the online product displays, adjusting prices, or mixing some of them? Prescriptive analytics can recommend the best course of action to enhance customer satisfaction.

Prescriptive analytics also has other applications that are critical to e-commerce businesses. Today's online customer experience is all about personalization. Therefore, online shops need to analyze customer data and target specific audiences with specific offers that encourage loyalty and increase conversions. Targeted marketing campaigns give an excellent example of how prescriptive analytics can help make shopping experiences unique for different groups of customers based on their demographic characteristics, purchasing behavior, and psychographic profiles. Demographic characteristics refer to basic customer features such as age, gender, and income level. Purchasing behavior includes attributes like frequency of purchase, average order value, product category preferences, and channel preferences (i.e., purchase through websites, mobile apps, or social media platforms). Psychographic profiles capture other attributes that may help companies differentiate targeted customers. For example, some customers are always passionate about staying updated on the latest trends and clothing styles. They often purchase limited edition items but are not too sensitive to high price tags. In contrast, some other customers may be budget-conscious shoppers who prioritize value for money and are more inclined to purchase items on sale. One other customer segment could be those who are environmentally conscious. They consistently seek organic materials and eco-friendly clothing collections.

After identifying high-value customer groups with unique preferences and needs, the retailer can effectively tailor marketing campaigns and promotional offers to target each segment. For example, prescriptive analytics may recommend sending personalized emails about new, limited edition products to customers who are enthusiastic about the latest trends. Loyal budget-conscious shoppers should receive exclusive discounts and loyalty rewards if they meet a certain spending criterion each year. Furthermore, highlighting sustainable initiatives and transparent sourcing practices can attract environmentally conscious customers.

While prescriptive analytics is powerful in finding an optimal solution, it is noteworthy that an algorithm is only as good as the input it gets. Human judgment is still essential in selecting an appropriate algorithm and validating various inputs and assumptions fed into the algorithm.

The subsequent section will focus on key considerations in applying prescriptive analytics for optimizing supply chain responses based on customer preferences, offering insights that extend beyond the women's clothing e-commerce data scenario.

4.3   Optimizing Supply Chain Responses Based on Customer Preferences

In the supply chain management (SCM) domain, there is a vast body of knowledge on optimizing service parts logistics, which form the core of service systems that support essential equipment at customer sites. These service systems and customer operations critically rely on the timely availability of service parts. The service expectations are based on service contracts defining fill rates and service time. For example, 80% of the service requests, i.e., delivery or installation of a service part, should be satisfied within a 2-h window, and 90% of the service requests should be met within a 4-h window. Any delay in the service of a failed critical system, such as a banking computer server, can have significant financial consequences for the customer. The fill rate and service time requirements pose a complex inventory management problem, requiring decisions on how many units to store and where to store in a highly distributed network [1]. However, using Mixed Integer and Nonlinear Programming (MINLP) models, service providers can optimally plan the inventory (inventory policy parameters) and logistics (location and distribution) based on the service contracts.

In the retail context, even though the time requirements are not strict, the coexistence of online and brick-and-mortar channels and their interfaces have significantly increased the complexity of downstream inventory and logistics management. In the apparel industry, for example, a customer may desire the flexibility of omnichannel, which can be defined as an integrated multichannel approach to sales [2]. The level of service a customer perceives can depend on the product availability and channel flexibility. As there are no contractual understandings with customers, the knowledge of customer preferences for products and channels gained from descriptive and predictive analytics can play an important role in customer service level.

The omnichannel retailing model aims to develop a synergetic management of various available channels and customer touchpoints to optimize the customer experience and the retailer's performance over multiple channels [2, 3]. It combines retail models such as click and collect, buy-online-pickup-in-store, reserve-online-pickup-in-store, buy-in-store-ship-home, and buy-online-ship-home [4]. Besides allowing freedom to customers, the omnichannel model has advantages for retailers; e.g., retailers can use their in-store inventory efficiently and reduce the need for in-store markdowns. However, omnichannel management requires balancing the trade-off between serving online customers and ensuring an adequate service level to in-store customers [3]. It also involves the management of the trade-off between high product availability for customers in all channels and overstocking [5]. Besides addressing questions like where to locate the stores, where to keep the stocks, and in what sequence to plan the deliveries [4], omnichannel optimization can guide managers on how to decide on the amount of inventory to replenish and the percentage to reserve for online orders [3]. The optimization, in turn, can be guided by the knowledge of customer preferences.

Efficient capturing of customer preferences and demand trends can also lead to streamlined and agile upstream processes. SHEIN, a China-based retail platform, offers a remarkable example of using information technology and artificial intelligence (AI) to match consumer demand to design and disperse production. Its response to evolving demand trends is multiple times faster than the fast-fashion icons such as Zara and H&M. In 2021, SHEIN developed 20 times as many new items as H&M or Zara [6]. Through what it calls the Large-Scale Automated Test and Reorder (LATR) model (Fig. 4.11), SHEIN connects its large consumer base in North America and Europe with around 6000 clothing factories in China. These small factories originally served the North American and European markets indirectly through mass merchants such as Walmart, and, as a result, could only make a small profit. With the advent of e-commerce platforms like Amazon, Chinese businesses are able to create a more direct channel in the Western markets, but understanding and responding to fast-changing consumer tastes is difficult. SHEIN, primarily based on its strong IT and AI capabilities, overcomes both challenges, i.e., providing a direct channel in the Western markets and understanding and responding to the demand dynamics in a very responsive manner. SHEIN has acquired a

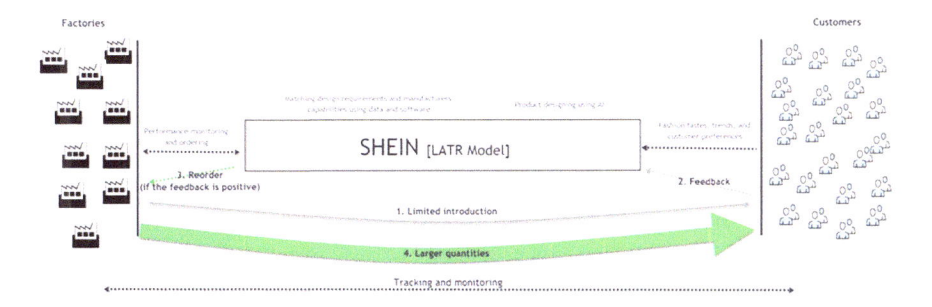

Fig. 4.11 SHEIN's Large-Scale Automated Test and Reorder (LATR) Model

deep sense of the fashion tastes of its consumers. It uses AI technology to identify trends [7], and when it sees potential in a design, it commissions a small order from its suppliers. It floats a limited quantity on its channels to gauge customer interest. If the customer response is positive, SHEIN reorders more. SHEIN uses data and software to align designs with the capabilities of particular producers in its manufacturing network. Manufacturer performance and customer preferences are also closely monitored. Essentially, one face of the LATR model captures customer preferences and tests SHEIN's offerings, while the other face engages thousands of production facilities to respond to customer preferences efficiently [6].

The "SHEIN way" can provide potential learning for industries other than fashion retail to leverage information and AI technologies to play a more significant and efficient role in connecting customer demand and supply base. As mentioned above, prescriptive models can provide valuable insights to facilitate optimum location, distribution, and inventory decisions to serve customers, but the efficacy of these models can be dependent on knowledge of customer preferences. LATR-like models can play a crucial role in this regard. IT and AI capabilities can create an ecosystem to capture demand dynamics in real time and enable the best configuration of supply chain operations even when intermediaries are involved. The same capabilities can allow timely detection and mitigation of supply chain disruptions.

References

1. Jat, M. N. (2018). Optimizing area coverage for time-differentiated distribution: A unidimensional analysis. *Transportation Journal, 57*(1), 83–111. https://doi.org/10.5325/transportationj.57.1.0083
2. Verhoef, P. C., Kannan, P. K., & Inman, J. J. (2015). From multi-channel retailing to omnichannel retailing: Introduction to the special issue on multi-channel retailing. *Journal of Retailing, 91*(2), 174–181. https://doi.org/10.1016/j.jretai.2015.02.005
3. Xu, J., & Cao, L. (2019). Optimal in-store inventory policy for omnichannel retailers in franchising networks. *International Journal of Retail & Distribution Management, 47*(12), 1251–1265. https://doi.org/10.1108/IJRDM-09-2018-0199
4. Saghiri, S., Aktas, E., & Mohammadipour, M. (2023). Grocery omnichannel perishable inventories: Performance measures and influencing factors. *International Journal of Operations & Production Management, 43*(12), 1891–1919. https://doi.org/10.1108/IJOPM-06-2022-0397
5. Perera, H. N., Fahimnia, B., & Tokar, T. (2020). Inventory and ordering decisions: A systematic review on research-driven through behavioral experiments. *International Journal of Operations and Production Management, 40*(7/8), 997–1039. https://doi.org/10.1108/IJOPM-05-2019-0339
6. Deighton, J. (2023, April 25). How SHEIN and Temu conquered fast fashion—and forged a new business model. Retrieved September 8, 2023, from https://hbswk.hbs.edu/item/how-shein-and-temu-conquered-fast-fashion-and-forged-a-new-business-model
7. Dawkins, J. O. & Mayer, G. (2023, November 28). Shein has filed to go public and is reportedly seeking up to $90 billion valuation. Here's how Shein Chartered a Meteoric Rise. Retrieved November 30, 2023, from https://www.businessinsider.com/what-is-shein-billion-dollar-fast-fashion-company-explained-2023-7#customer-hauls-on-tiktok-made-shein-a-huge-success-4

Chapter 5
Future of Customer-Centric Service-Based Supply Chains

5.1 Preamble

As discussed throughout this text, businesses in the twenty-first-century supply chain are witnessing one of the most dramatic technological transformations in the history of humanity. The ongoing tectonic shift brought on by Industry 4.0 has indeed started a revolution that is complex, inclusive, and automated. As mentioned in Chap. 1, the convergence of physical technology (e.g., IoT devices, sensors and actuators, and edge devices) and digital technology (artificial intelligence (AI), machine learning (ML), big data analytics (BDA), blockchain technologies (BCT), etc.) is expected to create fully integrated CPS, which can actively interact with each other. The speed of the resulting digital transformation occurring in every aspect of the economic, social, and personal arenas has developed the notion that we may be passing through the early stages of technological singularity [1], spurring ongoing debates among scientists and technology CEOs regarding data governance of the advancements, along with the discussion on the need for a dependable system of accountability vs an independent system of autonomy.

As we envision the future of CCSSC, powered by constant innovation in data science, to deliver personalized products, services, and experiences, we anticipate the emergence of enhanced technologies that enable CPS to generate, collect, store, and analyze large quantities of complex datasets. Future CCSSC should also require a continuous update of the knowledge base and infrastructure capable of providing checks and balances concerning data security, privacy, ethics, and governance.

P. S. Kang et al., *Service 4.0*, SpringerBriefs in Service Science, https://doi.org/10.1007/978-3-031-63875-6_5

5.2 Opportunities

In Chap. 3, we highlighted how the scope and capabilities of BDA could be elevated by incorporating blockchain-based applications in CCSSC. The business value added in the future for BCT-driven initiatives is vast in domains such as government, banking, healthcare, supply chain (SC) and logistics, legal, and disaster relief operations, to name a few [2]. One of the most promising areas of BCT use cases, however, can be discovered in BDA. Combining the synergistic effects of BCT and BDA will unleash a wide array of opportunities in data management as the sheer quantity and complexity of data increases. The most prominent advantage of BCT-based BDA is that BCT complements and fixes shortcomings inherent in BDA by rendering the data more valuable, secure, and trustworthy. These technologies can collectively enhance decision-making processes, optimize inventory management, and accurately forecast demand patterns.

5.2.1 Growth Potential: Blockchain Technology-Based Big Data Analytics

Data from different sources reveal gaps in their projection of the global blockchain and BDA market sizes, respectively. However, their expected trajectories or the compound annual growth rates (CAGR) show similar results.

- Global BCT market:

    - Statista: The business value of the global BCT market was estimated at $5.85 billion in 2021. BCT market size in 2030 is forecasted to reach $1.236 trillion, representing a CAGR of 82.8% over the period [3].
    - Gartner Research: The business value generated by the global BCT market will reach $176 billion by 2025 and $3.1 trillion by 2030, representing a CAGR of 77.5% [4].

- Global BDA market:

    - Statista: BDA's global market value was over $240 billion in 2021. The market value is expected to reach over $650 billion by 2029, exhibiting a CAGR of 13.3% [5].
    - Fortune Business Insights: The global BDA market size is projected to grow from $308 billion in 2023 to $745 billion by 2030, showing a CAGR of 13.5% during the forecast period [6].

It should be noted that the projected global BCT market size reflects the combined business value of all BCT-based projects. Considering BCT application is still nascent, the explosive growth forecast made by various sources on the global BCT market size is a plausible scenario, especially with the rapid adoption of other Industry 4.0 technologies across different sectors.

In particular, the amalgamation of BCT and BDA is expected to carry a powerful impact beyond the mere linking of the two technologies: the recent advent of Big Data-as-a-Service (BdaaS) and Blockchain-as-a-Service (BaaS) has revealed the combined capability to transform CCSSC to a system with an enhanced level of data integrity based on transparency, reliability, and trust [7–9]. This can potentially have a transformative impact beyond individual companies or sectors. Collaboration among different industries, stakeholders, and regulatory bodies is imperative to create unified standards, share best practices, and address challenges collectively. Cross-industry collaboration can accelerate the adoption of these technologies and ensure a more cohesive and interoperable SC ecosystem.

The future of CCSSC can be viewed as a multifaceted journey, marked by the convergence of BCT, BDA, AI, ML, and other Industry 4.0 technologies. While the discussed elements lay the foundation, the industry's dynamic nature requires ongoing exploration and adaptation to emerging trends and challenges. Keeping abreast of these developments will be vital for companies seeking to establish resilient, transparent, and customer-centric supply chain ecosystems.

5.3 Challenges and Limitations

5.3.1 The Blockchain Trilemma

BCT is often touted as the game-changer of data governance [2]. In essence, BCT's trusted sharing principle of data governance advocates decentralization, scalability, and security, which, in turn, should lead to system-wide transparency and trust in CCSSC. Ideally, these three core features of BCT must be satisfied simultaneously, as compromising even a single feature among the three may result in undesirable consequences such as data breaches and governance risks associated with malicious attacks [10]. The inevitable trade-off observed among the three core features of BCT is called "the blockchain trilemma" as displayed in Fig. 5.1, referring to the difficulties faced by blockchain-based systems in achieving optimal levels of three features at the same time.

Typically, security (e.g., the ability of a data network to defend against malicious attacks) hinders scalability (e.g., difficulties in handling large volumes of data), scalability limits decentralization (e.g., the dispersion of supervision of data away from a single point of control), and decentralization compromises security.

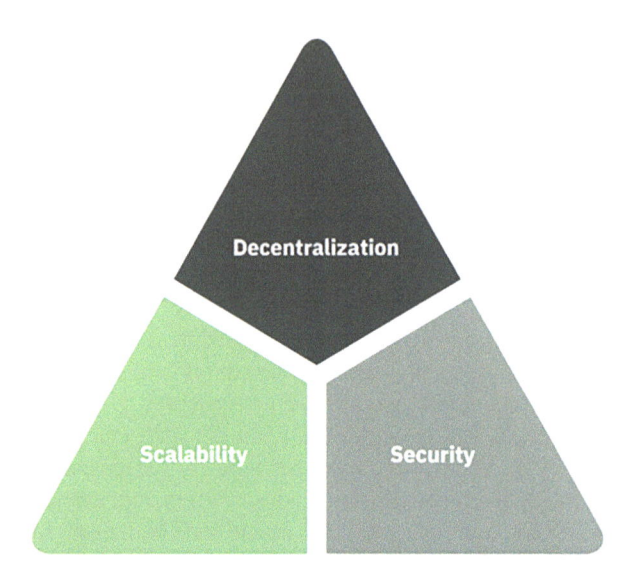

Fig. 5.1 The blockchain trilemma (https://www.electraprotocol.com/knowledgebase/blockchain-trilemma/)

5.3.2 Data Privacy and Security

Due to the blockchain trilemma, most of the active blockchains in use focus only on one or two core features at the expense of the third, as exemplified in blockchains in the food supply chain (mainly focused on security and scalability), pharmaceutical industry (focused on security), and supply chain finance (focused on security) [11]. The lack of decentralization focus in active blockchain systems leads to primarily permissioned blockchain types currently in use (i.e., either private or consortium blockchain), driven by concerns about possible attacks on data privacy and security [9]. The preference for a permissioned blockchain, where access to data is granted selectively to known parties only, is a clear display of priority by data users for data privacy and security over the other two core features [12]. It is noted, however, that this may come at the expense of data integrity, which is achievable by the decentralization feature of BCT.

In recent years, some progress has been made with zero-knowledge proofs or zero-knowledge protocols (ZKPs) to upgrade the data privacy and security of BCT-based data management while upholding the decentralization feature. A ZKP is a cryptographic technology by which one party (the prover) can prove a claim to another party (the verifier) without revealing other information beyond the validity of the claim itself (Fig. 5.2) [13].

The central premise of ZKPs is that it is relatively trivial to prove the possession of certain information by revealing it; however, it is challenging to prove such possession without exposing the information itself [14]. In essence, ZKPs must demonstrate completeness, soundness, and zero-knowledge properties in the process [15].

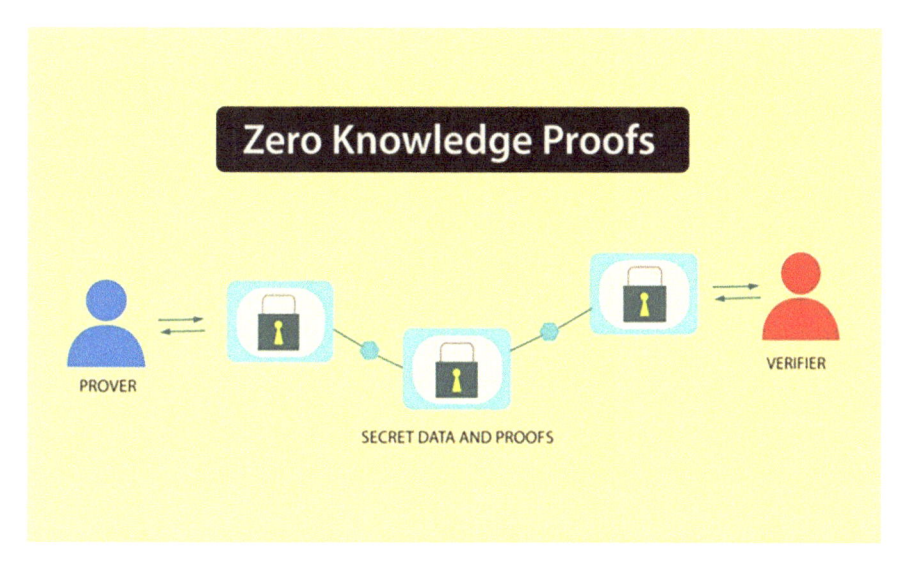

Fig.   5.2 Zero-knowledge   proofs   (https://www.itsecuritydemand.com/insights/security/a-comprehensive-guide-to-zero-knowledge-proofs-zkps/)

In supply chain management, where data sharing and interactions with other partners are common, ZKPs are recognized for their potential to safeguard data privacy in various contexts and processes as follows:

- Validation of product authenticity: Using blockchain-enabled ZKPs, the supplier can prove the authenticity of goods without disclosing its proprietary manufacturing process or the details of parts and components. Further, the privacy-preserving authentication protocols of ZKPs are often employed to securely verify user credentials in multi-party transactions in the supply chain, enhancing transaction integrity. It is crucial that only authorized parties have access to permissioned supply chain blockchain networks [16].
- Data privacy in smart contract execution: Blockchain applications are capable of separating sensitive information generated along the supply chain. For instance, the IBM Food Trust, a partnership with Walmart, requires minimal sharing of sensitive information, such as inventory storage, payments, and purchase orders [12]. In cases where sensitive data needs to be shared and processed when executing smart contracts in the supply chain, BCT-based ZKPs are used to enable secure and private transactions to maintain a high level of trust among the stakeholders.
- Supply chain collaboration: ZKPs are essential for enabling secure multi-party collaboration, which may entail joint computations using private datasets. ZKPs offer a secure means of data sharing during the collaborative process, protecting the confidentiality of sensitive information of stakeholders [17].
- Supply chain traceability and provenance: Supply chains often require tracking the provenance of products, including the inventory flows and the transfer of

ownership. In the process, each touchpoint in the journey needs to be verified and recorded on the blockchain. ZKPs can be used to verify the current status of a product and its handling by authorized parties without disclosing the location, the delivery route, or other sensitive information about the parties involved. In particular, this feature is highly relevant in cases where traceability is essential, such as in food and pharmaceutical supply chains [18, 19].

- Compliance verification: Meeting compliance standards is often a critical requirement in the supply chain. ZKPs help companies maintain confidentiality in demonstrating compliance with ethical and sustainable standards in their business practices without undermining the competitive advantages of their operations [18, 20].

Data privacy has been one of the main factors broadly holding back enterprise adoption of public blockchain technology. By incorporating ZKPs, organizations can strike a balance between transparency and privacy, addressing concerns related to data privacy, security, and confidentiality while safeguarding the decentralization feature of public blockchain [16].

5.3.3 Other Issues

While the core features of blockchain are appealing in their potential contribution to enhanced integrity and the security of the BDA ecosystem, they could easily become a double-edged sword, exposing organizations and data users to complicated problems with ethical, legal, and financial ramifications [21], such as lack of a central party protection or reliance on the ethical standards of anonymous parties. The value of data management in CCSSC is maximized when evidence-based data-driven decisions provide novel opportunities to utilize and combine new digital technologies for the future ecosystem.

Amid the ongoing digital transformation that has impacted every organization, one key principle still holds the people, process, and technology (PPT) framework. As seen in Fig. 5.3, at the highest level, it is the people (who) who design the process (how) to implement the technology solution (what). Unlike the blockchain trilemma, the priority set forth in the PPT principle should not be compromised.

- People (Who): People bring essential skills, knowledge, and adaptability, which are central to the success of any digital transformation initiative by embracing the change and fostering a culture of innovation. In the context of CCSSC, the role of people extends beyond internal teams to encompass collaborative efforts across SC partners and stakeholders.
- Process (How): In the context of CCSSC, this involves reimagining traditional SC processes with a focus on efficiency, transparency, and responsiveness. The integration of BCT and BDA necessitates reevaluating existing processes to harness the full potential of these technologies. It also involves establishing robust

Fig. 5.3 People–process–technology (PPT) framework (https://www.echoprojectmanagement.com/post/balancing-people-process-and-technology-1)

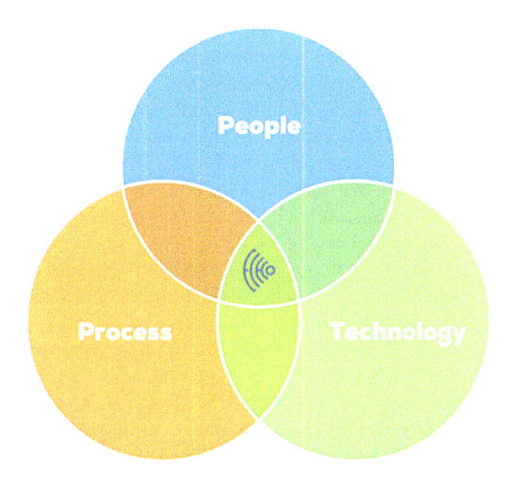

governance structures, ensuring compliance, and adapting to dynamic market conditions.

- Technology (What): The integration of BCT, BDA, AI, ML, and other Industry 4.0 technologies becomes the technological backbone. BCT and BDA, with their capabilities in providing transparency, security, and power to derive actionable insights, can potentially make them an integral component of CCSSC and exemplify the evolving technological landscape within CCSSC.

References

1. Shanahan, M. (2015). *The technological singularity*. The MIT Press.
2. Manzoor, R., Sahay, B. S., & Singh, S. K. (2022). Blockchain technology in supply chain management: An organizational theoretic overview and research agenda. *Annals of Operations Research*. https://doi.org/10.1007/s10479-022-05069-5
3. Statista. (n.d.). Blockchain technology market size worldwide in 2021, with a forecast for 2030. Retrieved November 10, 2023, from https://www.statista.com/statistics/1319369/global-blockchain-technology-market-size/
4. Gartner Research. (n.d.). Digital disruption profile: Blockchain's radical promise spans business and society. Retrieved November 10, 2023, from https://www.gartner.com/en/doc/3855708-digital-disruption-profile-blockchains-radical-promise-spans-business-and-society
5. Statista. (n.d.). Size of the big data analytics market worldwide from 2021 to 2029. Retrieved November 10, 2023, from https://www.statista.com/statistics/1336002/big-data-analytics-market-size/
6. Fortune Business Insights. (n.d.). Big data analytics market size, share, and COVID-19 impact analysis, 2023–2030. Retrieved November 10, 2023, from https://www.fortunebusinessinsights.com/big-data-analytics-market-106179
7. Sundarakani, B., Ajaykumar, A., & Gunasekaran, A. (2021). Big data driven supply chain design and applications for blockchain: An action research using case study approach. *Omega, 102,* 102452. https://doi.org/10.1016/j.omega.2021.102452

8. Liu, J., Zhao, H., Lyu, Y., & Yue, X. (2023). The provision strategy of blockchain service under the supply chain with downstream competition. *Annals of Operations Research, 327*, 375–400. https://doi.org/10.1007/s10479-022-05034-2

9. Narwane, V. S., Raut, R. D., Mangla, S. K., Dora, M., & Narkhede, B. E. (2023). Blockchain in operations and supply chain management. *Annals of Operations Research, 327*, 339–374. https://doi.org/10.1007/s10479-023-05451-x

10. Reno, S., & Haque, M. M. (2023). Solving blockchain trilemma using off-chain storage protocol. *The Institution of Engineering and Technology Information Society, 17*, 681–702. https://doi.org/10.1049/ise2.12124

11. Teoh, B. P. C. (2022). Chapter 25. Navigating the blockchain trilemma: A supply chain dilemma. In A. Ismail, W. M. Dahalan, & A. Öchsner (Eds.), *Advanced maritime technologies and applications* (pp. 291–300).

12. Gaur, V., & Gaiha, A. (2020). Building a transparent supply chain. *Harvard Business Review, 98*(2), 94–103.

13. Berentsen, A., Lenzi, J., & Nyffenegger, R. (2023). An introduction to zero-knowledge proofs in blockchains and economics. *Federal Reserve Bank of St. Louis Review, 105*(4), 280–294.

14. Goldreich, O. (2001). *Foundations of cryptography* (Vol. I, pp. 184–330). Cambridge University Press. https://doi.org/10.1017/CBO9780511546891.005

15. Feige, U., Fiat, A., & Shamir, A. (1988). Zero-knowledge proofs of identity. *Journal of Cryptology, 1*, 77–94. https://doi.org/10.1007/BF02351717

16. Zhou, L., Diro, A., Saini, A., Kaisar, S., & Hiep, P. C. (2024). Leveraging zero knowledge proofs for blockchain-based identity sharing: A survey of advancements, challenges and opportunities. *Journal of Information Security and Applications, 80*, 103678. https://doi.org/10.1016/j.jisa.2023.103678

17. Ben-Sasson, E., Chiesa, A., Garman, C., Green, M., Miers, I., Tromer, E., & Virza, M. (2014). Zerocash: Decentralized anonymous payments from Bitcoin. In *2014 IEEE symposium on security and privacy* (pp. 459–474). https://doi.org/10.1109/SP.2014.36

18. Prasad, S., Tiwari, N., Chawla, M., & Tomar, D. S. (2024). Zero-knowledge proofs in blockchain-enabled supply chain management. In A. Kumar, N. J. Ahuja, K. Kaushik, D. S. Tomar, & S. B. Khan (Eds.), *Sustainable security practices using blockchain, quantum and post-quantum technologies for real time applications*. Springer. https://doi.org/10.1007/978-981-97-0088-2_3

19. Lei, M., Xu, L., Liu, T., Liu, S., & Sun, C. (2022). Integration of privacy protection and blockchain-based food safety traceability: Potential and challenges. *Food, 11*(15), 2262. https://doi.org/10.3390/foods11152262

20. Chainlink. (2023). Zero-knowledge proofs: Applications and use cases. Retrieved April 2, 2024, from https://chain.link/education-hub/zero-knowledge-proof-use-cases

21. Blackman, R. (2022). Why blockchain's ethical stakes are so high. *Harvard Business Review*. Available at: https://hbr.org/2022/05/why-blockchains-ethical-stakes-are-so-high.